PRAISE | T0012811

SUN SIGNS, HOUSE⌐ ⌐ ⌐⌐⌐⌐⌐⌐

"An illuminating introduction to healing through astrology. Carmen Turner-Schott deftly explains the basics of astrology, demystifies the theory and terminology of the practice, and helps us with strategies for healing. *Sun Signs, Houses & Healing* is organized into easy-to-use sections, helping the reader understand the strengths and challenges of each sign ... A welcome addition to the spiritual reader's library!"

—Mara Bishop, MA, author of
Shamanism for Every Day and *Inner Divinity*

"A unique, magical alchemy guiding the reader to paths filled with transformation. What makes this book extra special is that the author, Carmen Turner-Schott, translates the complex language of astrology into information that can instantly be put to practical use ... The author's many years of counseling experience shine through the pages and offer a positive way to perceive the world ... It is a book each of us needs as a close companion."

—Bernie Ashman, author of *Sun Sign Karma*

SUN SIGNS
HOUSES
& HEALING

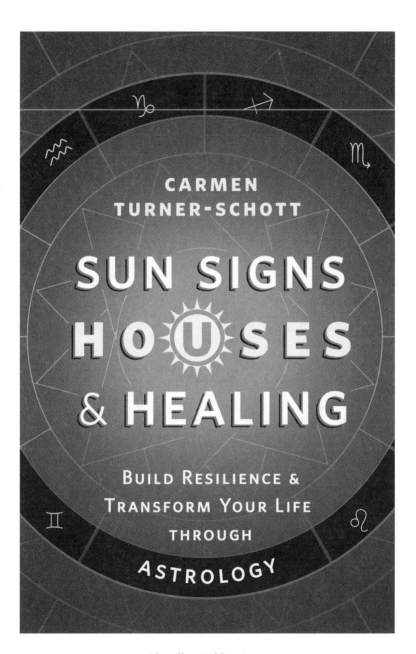

CARMEN
TURNER-SCHOTT

SUN SIGNS
HO☉SES
& HEALING

BUILD RESILIENCE &
TRANSFORM YOUR LIFE
THROUGH
ASTROLOGY

Llewellyn Publications
Woodbury, Minnesota

FIRST EDITION
First Printing, 2022

Book design by Valerie A. King
Cover design by Shira Atakpu

Birth chart illustration on page 5 from Astro Dienst, www.astro.com

Llewellyn Publications is a registered trademark of Llewellyn Worldwide Ltd.

Library of Congress Cataloging-in-Publication Data
Names: Turner-Schott, Carmen, author.
Title: Sun signs, houses & healing : build resilience and transform your
   life through astrology / Carmen Turner-Schott.
Other titles: Sun signs, houses and healing
Description: First edition. | Woodbury, Minnesota : Llewellyn Publications,
   2022. | Summary: "This beginner-friendly book provides crucial insights
   on all twelve signs and reveals how your personality traits help you
   overcome challenges and improve well-being" —Provided by publisher.
Identifiers: LCCN 2022000160 (print) | LCCN 2022000161 (ebook) | ISBN
   9780738771304 | ISBN 9780738771588 (ebook)
Subjects: LCSH: Astrology.
Classification: LCC BF1708.1 .T84 2022 (print) | LCC BF1708.1 (ebook) |
   DDC 133.5—dc23/eng/20220208
LC record available at https://lccn.loc.gov/2022000160
LC ebook record available at https://lccn.loc.gov/2022000161

Llewellyn Publications
A Division of Llewellyn Worldwide Ltd.
2143 Wooddale Drive
Woodbury, MN 55125-2989
www.llewellyn.com

Printed in the United States of America

OTHER BOOKS BY CARMEN TURNER-SCHOTT

A Deeper Look at the Sun Signs

A Practical Look at the Planets in the Houses

Astrology Awareness

Astrology from a Christian Perspective

The Mysteries of the Eighth Astrological House

FORTHCOMING BOOKS BY CARMEN TURNER-SCHOTT

The Mysteries of the Twelfth Astrological House

Phoenixes and Angels

© Janice Kay Turner

About the Author

Carmen Turner-Schott, MSW, LISW, is a practicing clinical social worker, writer, and astrologer with national and international clientele. She graduated from Washington University in St. Louis with a Master of Social Work degree in 1999. She currently works as a Sexual Assault Prevention and Response Program Manager and has worked with victims of trauma for over twenty-five years.

Carmen began her astrological work at the age of sixteen, after an experience with a glowing ball of light in her doorway. She began studying religion, astrology, and metaphysics at that time. She has lectured and presented astrology workshops and eGroups for the Association of Research and Enlightenment (A.R.E.). She also enjoys teaching a variety of spiritual development classes.

For the past twenty-five years, Carmen has been researching astrology, transformation, and healing. She founded the Astrological Self Awareness Center in 2005 and later changed the name to Deep Soul Divers Astrology. She has a passion for researching astrology and specializes in the eighth and twelfth astrological houses and their effects on trauma, healing, and resiliency.

She has self-published five astrology books, *The Mysteries of the Eighth Astrological House: Phoenix Rising, A Deeper Look at the Sun Signs, A Practical Look at the Planets in the Houses, Astrology from a Christian Perspective,* and *Astrology Awareness: A Compilation of Articles.* You can learn more about Carmen at www.8and 12houses.com, www.facebook.com/CarmenTurnerSchottWriter/, and www.facebook.com/deepsouldiversastrology/.

This book is dedicated to all those who seek greater self-awareness through astrology.

I cherish all the members of my astrological Facebook groups, consisting of members from all over the world, and I am thankful for your support, stories, and collaboration.

I want to thank my mentor, friend, and fellow astrologer, "Bernie Ashman," for his continued belief in me, my work, and my writing, and for encouraging me through many difficult times.

CONTENTS

INTRODUCTION

E veryone can benefit from healing and transforming themselves. In this book we are going to discuss how each of the
twelve signs of the zodiac utilize their personality traits to accomplish three things: transformation, healing, and resiliency. Let's
begin by talking about self-care and why healing is so important.

WHAT IS SELF-CARE?

Self-care is making a conscious effort to take care of the body,
mind, and spirit. It is not something that is done only once; it's
a routine that needs to be developed in everyday life. Self-care
helps prevent burnout, reduces the effects of stress, and helps us
reflect on what is important in our lives. Examples of self-care
are taking breaks, healthy eating, exercising, asking for help,
spending time alone, putting yourself first, setting boundaries,
forgiving yourself, and enjoying hobbies.

The reason self-care techniques do not work the same way
for everyone is because of the unique way the elements in our
birth chart affect our ability to react to stress, heal, relax, and
recharge. Self-care tips work differently for each sun sign. Those

with similar elements will benefit from similar activities. Gaining a deeper understanding of yourself and thinking about what activities help you recharge are important parts of self-care. This book will help you on your self-care journey.

THE BENEFITS OF HEALING

We all heal in different ways, and it takes some of us longer to fully heal from past experiences. Learning to balance the body, mind, and spirit is a key factor in the healing process. Everyone has different abilities and strengths that help them bounce back after a crisis.

There are many benefits to focusing on healing. Healing helps us grow stronger by letting go of negative emotions and experiences. Healing allows us to redefine ourselves and reclaim our power. Addressing past wounds helps us transform and find greater happiness. Many of us carry unhealed trauma and emotions within our bodies that can manifest as physical illness, stress, or anxiety if unaddressed for too long.

The greatest thing about healing is that when we address our own pain, we can become role models for others on their healing journey. Greater insight occurs when we are able to identify our emotional issues, problem-solve, and discuss our experiences with those we care about. Sometimes it can take longer than expected to truly move forward from past experiences. Everyone heals at their own pace. Be patient with yourself.

SUN SIGNS & HEALING

Each sun sign experiences change and stress, so implementing self-care techniques will benefit you regardless of your sign.

With that being said, understanding your basic sun sign traits is a powerful tool for healing many areas of life. When you flip to the chapter on your sun sign, this book will shed light on your overall personality and discuss ways to overcome challenges.

In the following chapters, I explain the basic personality traits of each sun sign. I discuss each sun sign's challenging attributes, positive attributes, and how they approach relationships. These chapters are great tools for learning more about yourself and your loved ones. If you want to learn more about your family, friends, or coworkers, read their sun sign's chapter.

In each chapter, I include reflection questions, affirmations, and self-care ideas tailored to that specific sign. You can use these on your healing journey. I then discuss which house that sun sign rules and how placements in that house impact us.

This might sound overwhelming if you are new to astrology. So first, let's cover some astrological basics.

ASTROLOGY & YOUR BIRTH CHART

Astrology is what I call a map of the soul. By studying astrology, you can learn to read birth charts, including your own.

WHAT IS A BIRTH CHART?

Everyone has a birth chart. It is an image of the astrological and planetary placements at your exact moment of birth. Like a fingerprint, it is totally unique to you. Your birth chart reveals your main personality traits, your emotional nature, how you think, how you love, what type of careers you are drawn to, any psychic abilities you may possess, areas you tend to struggle with, your overall childhood experience, your relationship with your parents, your past lives, and your current soul mission. By analyzing your birth chart's planetary and house placements, you can learn anything you want to know about yourself. In this book, we are sticking to sun signs and house placements. Learning more about your sun sign will help validate things about yourself. Basic personality astrology is powerful and can be used as a tool for greater self-awareness.

To calculate a birth chart or natal chart, you need to know three things: the individual's date of birth, the exact time they were born, and the place where they were born. When you calculate a birth chart, it is important to know the exact time of birth because the time of birth is crucial to calculating an accurate birth chart. For instance, my husband and I were born on the same day, August 26, but we were born in different years and at different times. Anyone born on August 26 will be a Virgo sun, but the year, location of birth, and time of birth will affect which houses and signs the other planets are placed in. Even twins can have slightly different personalities, especially if the time of birth is different.

When you calculate a birth chart, you will see a wheel divided into twelve sections. Birth charts will be overwhelming at first because there are lots of symbols, lines, and colors on the chart. Feeling overwhelmed is totally normal. To begin reading the birth chart, locate the numbers one through twelve in the wheel. These numbers denote the twelve sections, or houses, a birth chart is divided into.

Find the number one, which will be on the left side of the chart. The first house is the beginning of a birth chart. Look for the zodiac sign that is named on the rim of the first house. This

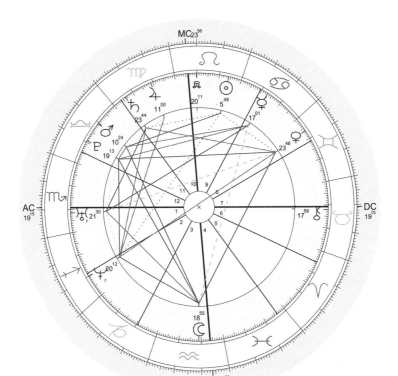

zodiac sign is the sign that was on the horizon at the time of birth. It is known as the *ascendant* or *rising sign* and officially starts the first house. Time of birth is crucial because rising signs change every two hours, and an inaccurate rising sign will affect the accuracy of every other house in a birth chart.

The birth chart's twelve houses move counterclockwise from the first house. Once you know where to begin, you can see which sign rules your second house, third house, and so forth. A birth chart will show which houses and signs the planets are placed in. The planets are symbolized by images called *glyphs*. You will need to know the basic symbols to be able to determine which sign and house each planet is placed in. For the purposes of this book, we will be working with the sun's planetary placement, denoted by a circle with a dot in the middle. For instance, the birth wheel below shows someone who has a Scorpio rising (the first house begins in Scorpio) and has the sun in Leo in the ninth house.

Not every house in a birth chart will have planets in it, but each house will be ruled by one of the twelve astrological signs. The sign that rules the house can tell you something about the individual, and the planets placed in that sign can deepen that understanding.

It's totally normal for this information to be confusing; it will make more sense as we go. Now let's discuss the astrological signs in a bit more detail.

WHAT ARE THE TWELVE ZODIAC SIGNS?

There are twelve signs in the zodiac. They are Aries, Taurus, Gemini, Cancer, Leo, Virgo, Libra, Scorpio, Sagittarius, Capricorn, Aquarius, and Pisces. One of these signs will be your sun sign, calculated by the month and day of your birth. This is the only planetary placement that shifts with our traditional calendar, making it easy to determine. This is why so many people are familiar with their sun sign. An important note: If your birth took place on a date when the sun was in between zodiac signs or was very close to switching signs, astrologers call this being born on the *cusp*. If you were born on a cusp, you might resonate with traits of both signs. For instance, if you were born on January 19, then you might have personality traits of both

Capricorns and Aquarians. Typically, the sign the sun is moving into shows dominance and strength. If you're unsure of your sun sign, your birth chart can confirm that for you.

Each astrological sign has many components that make it unique: the sign's element, modality, ruler, and symbol. I'll now discuss each of these in detail. There will be a chart at the end of the section that sums up this information for easier reference.

Each sign is ruled by a certain natural element. The four elements that exist in nature are fire, air, earth, and water. Fire signs are full of energy and passion; they are Aries, Leo, and Sagittarius. Air signs—Gemini, Libra, and Aquarius—are intellectual and emotionally detached. Earth signs are practical and cautious; they are Taurus, Virgo, and Capricorn. Water signs are emotional and imaginative; Cancer, Scorpio, and Pisces are water signs.

Each sign is also categorized by a certain modality: cardinal, fixed, or mutable. A sign's modality is significant because it reveals a deeper part of their personality that others might not see. Cardinal signs are known to be self-motivated, ambitious, activity starters, and enthusiastic about new ideas. Fixed signs are determined, strong-willed, stable, and purposeful, and they dislike change. Mutable signs are known to be adaptable, changeable, versatile, and easygoing. When the element and modality are combined, this can tell you a lot about the sign. For example, Taurus is fixed earth. Knowing this tells you that Taurus is a reliable, determined sign that doesn't like change, because fixed signs are focused on stability and earth signs like to work hard to achieve their goals.

Each sign also has a planetary ruler. The ten planets are the sun, moon, Mercury, Venus, Mars, Jupiter, Saturn, Uranus, Neptune, and Pluto. Some signs share the same ruling planet.

- The sun rules Leo.

- The moon rules Cancer.

- Mercury rules Virgo and Gemini.

- Venus rules Libra and Taurus.

- Mars rules Aries.

- Jupiter rules Sagittarius.

- Saturn rules Capricorn.

- Uranus rules Aquarius.

- Neptune rules Pisces.

- Pluto rules Scorpio.

Don't worry, you're not expected to memorize this information. I will include more about each sun sign's planetary ruler in the following chapters.

When two signs share a planetary ruler—such as Virgo and Gemini, which are both ruled by Mercury—they are often attracted to each other. Both Virgos and Geminis feel comfortable communicating ideas, but the main difference is the element that rules them. Earth and air signs, for instance, are very different personality-wise. These two signs complement each other in the area of communication, but overall compatibility might be a challenge. Earth signs need stability, commitment, and organization, and air signs like excitement, change, and freedom. The signs Taurus and Libra also share a planetary ruler; they are both ruled by the planet Venus, making them both attractive, creative, and peaceful. They will have some similarities in their personality, but Taureans are very practical and focused on material things, whereas Libras are intellectual, focused on the mind and learning new things.

Each sign has an opposite sign that opposes it in the sky, and astrologers refer to this as the *polar opposite sign*. Polar opposite signs balance out each other's differences. Polar opposites are a compatible element because the two opposite signs complement each other. For instance, the constellation of Aries is always opposite the constellation of Libra in the sky. When reading the sun sign chapters, the polar opposite sign will be listed at the top of the chapter.

Each zodiac sign has special symbols associated with them. Aries is the first zodiac sign and is known as the ram. The second sign, Taurus, is the bull. The third sign, Gemini, is known as the twins. Cancer is the fourth sign and its symbol is the crab. Leo the lion is the fifth sign. The sixth sign is Virgo, the maiden. The seventh sign is Libra, represented by the scales of balance. Scorpio is associated with the scorpion. The ninth sign is Sagittarius the archer. Capricorn, represented by the goat, is the tenth sign. Aquarius is the eleventh sign and is known as the water bearer. The final sign of the zodiac is the twelfth sign, Pisces, known as the fish. All of these symbols will make sense once you've read about their corresponding sign.

The following is a chart that has all of the above information for easy reference.

Sign	Element	Modality	Planetary Ruler	Polar Opposite Sign	Symbol
Aries	Fire	Cardinal	Mars	Libra	The ram
Taurus	Earth	Fixed	Venus	Scorpio	The bull
Gemini	Air	Mutable	Mercury	Sagittarius	The twins
Cancer	Water	Cardinal	Moon	Capricorn	The crab
Leo	Fire	Fixed	Sun	Aquarius	The lion
Virgo	Earth	Mutable	Mercury	Pisces	The maiden
Libra	Air	Cardinal	Venus	Aries	The scales
Scorpio	Water	Fixed	Pluto	Taurus	The scorpion
Sagittarius	Fire	Mutable	Jupiter	Gemini	The archer
Capricorn	Earth	Cardinal	Saturn	Cancer	The goat
Aquarius	Air	Fixed	Uranus	Leo	The water bearer
Pisces	Water	Mutable	Neptune	Virgo	The fish

THE PLANETS AND THEIR MEANINGS

Traditionally, there are ten planets we need to focus on when analyzing a birth chart. The planets are the sun, moon, Mercury, Venus, Mars, Jupiter, Saturn, Uranus, Neptune, and Pluto. (Although the sun and moon are not technically planets in our solar system, they are considered a part of the personality in astrology, so throughout this book we will be referring to them as planets.)

The energy of each planet creates personality traits in the specific sign it rules. This book will highlight each sun sign's basic personality traits, the house associated with each sign, and what the planets mean in each house. Here is a planetary cheat sheet:

Glyph	Planet	Description
☉	Sun	Rules the sign Leo. The sun represents our main identity, personality, and ego. Symbolically, it also represents the father figure in a birth chart. The house where the sun is placed is where we like to shine.
☽	Moon	Rules the sign Cancer. The moon represents our emotional nature and inner life. The moon also represents the mother figure. How we express our feelings depends on which house and sign the moon is in.
☿	Mercury	Rules the signs Virgo and Gemini. Mercury represents thoughts, ideas, and the way we communicate. Wherever Mercury is placed is where we express ourself best, both through writing and speaking.
♀	Venus	Rules the signs Taurus and Libra. Venus represents our loving nature and values. Venus symbolizes the way we express our love and feelings. Wherever Venus is placed is where we experience and seek harmony.
♂	Mars	Rules the sign Aries. Mars represents our drive, energy, aggression, and impulses. Wherever Mars is placed is where we strive to succeed; it shows what we are very competitive about. It can also show where we experience conflict in life.

Glyph	Planet	Description
♃	Jupiter	Rules the sign Sagittarius. Jupiter represents luck, abundance, education, and travel. Jupiter shows where we benefit and experience good luck and fortune.
♄	Saturn	Rules the sign Capricorn. Saturn represents where we feel discipline and responsibility, as well as where we feel restricted. Wherever Saturn is placed in a birth chart is where we feel uncomfortable and limited. We must work hard to overcome this restricting energy.
♅	Uranus	Rules the sign Aquarius. Uranus represents our individuality and uniqueness. Anything unorthodox is Uranus energy. Uranus can represent sudden changes and the unexpected.
♆	Neptune	Rules the sign Pisces. Neptune represents spirituality, illusions, drugs, and music. Neptune shows where we find spirituality and where we can delude ourselves. It is associated with addiction, such as alcoholism or anything that helps us escape reality.
♇	Pluto	Rules the sign Scorpio. Pluto represents transformation and regeneration. Pluto is where we experience powerful spiritual and psychological changes within ourselves and the environment. Pluto is intense energy that is associated with sex, death, and other people's resources.

The energy of each planet is expressed more easily in some signs than others. Each planet is associated with a sun sign and is what is called a *planetary ruler*. The planet will feel totally at home when it is in the sign it rules, also called *domicile*, bringing positive energy. For instance, Mars rules Aries, so when it is placed in the sign Aries, it can express itself well.

Some planets are *exalted* in a sign. This simply means that the energy expresses itself easily and positively when the planet is placed in that sign. An example would be Venus in Pisces. Planets are in *detriment* when they are in the sign opposite of the one they rule; the sun rules Leo, so if the sun is in Aquarius, it is in detriment in the polar opposite sign. This means the planet might have trouble expressing its energy and true nature; it does not feel comfortable being placed in that sign. When a planet is in its *fall*, it means that it's very difficult for the planet to express itself at all. A planet in the sign opposite its exalted sign is in fall; this causes the planet to lose strength.

These planetary situations are what astrologers call *dignities*. Here is a bulleted list of the dignities for reference:

- Sun in Leo is domicile, detriment in Aquarius, exalted in Aries, and in fall when in Libra.

- Moon in Cancer is domicile, detriment in Capricorn, exalted in Taurus, and in fall when in Scorpio.

- Mercury in Virgo and Gemini is domicile, detriment in Sagittarius and Pisces, exalted in Virgo, and in fall when in Pisces.

- Venus in Taurus and Libra is domicile, detriment in Scorpio and Aries, exalted in Pisces, and in fall when in Virgo.

- Mars in Aries is domicile, detriment in Taurus and Libra, exalted in Capricorn, and in fall when in Cancer.

- Jupiter in Sagittarius is domicile, detriment in Gemini and Virgo, exalted in Cancer, and in fall when in Capricorn.

- Saturn in Capricorn is domicile, detriment in Cancer and Leo, exalted in Libra, and in fall when in Aries.

- Uranus in Aquarius is domicile, detriment in Leo, exalted in Scorpio, and in fall when in Taurus.

- Neptune in Pisces is domicile, detriment in Virgo, exalted in Cancer, and in fall when in Capricorn.

- Pluto in Scorpio is domicile, detriment in Taurus, exalted in Pisces, and in fall when in Virgo.

WHAT ARE THE TWELVE HOUSES?

The twelve houses in a birth chart represent significant areas of life. The houses are represented by sections of the sky. In the middle of the astrological wheel is the earth. Imagine standing inside that wheel and looking up at the sky. The sky is then divided into twelve sections, which are what astrologers call *houses*.

- **The first house** starts the birth wheel and represents our main personality, appearance, and identity. It is known as the *ascendant* or *rising sign*, and it creates the first impression we make in the world because it affects how others perceive us.

- **The second house** is the house of money, finances, and self-worth.

- **The third house** represents communication, siblings, and basic learning.

- **The fourth house** is the house of home and family. It is known as the *Imum Coeli* and sits at the bottom of the birth chart wheel.

- **The fifth house** is the house of children, creativity, pleasure, and fun.

- **The sixth house** is the house of work, routine, and health.

- **The seventh house** is known as the *descendant* and rules marriage and partnership.

- **The eighth house** is the house of death, healing, rebirth, trauma, and deep experiences.

- **The ninth house** is the house of travel, foreigners, higher education, and religion.

- **The tenth house** is the career house. It is known as the *midheaven* because it sits at the top of the birth chart wheel.

- **The eleventh house** represents friendship, groups, and humanitarian causes.

- **The twelfth house** is the house of sacrifice, spirituality, escapism, and service to others.

An easy way to remember the sign that rules each house is simple. Aries is the first zodiac sign and rules the first house. Taurus is the second sign and rules the second house, Gemini rules the third, and so on through Pisces.

Your personality is expressed through these areas of life based on which planets are placed in each house of the birth chart. Planets have a certain energy, so where they land in a birth chart is important because it shows how their energy affects that specific area of life. For example, if you are born in late October, then the sun was in Scorpio when you were born. Scorpios need to learn how to heal, dive deeply into life, develop intimacy, and trust others. The house where the Scorpio sun is placed will explain where and how these lessons influence life. So if the sun is in the second house, this Scorpio will be learning to trust others with finances, building lasting security, and developing stability to resist change. In summary, when you know the meaning of each planet and then look at which house it's in, you can see where that planet's energy makes an impact.

In the upcoming chapters about each house, I will describe people who have planets in a house a certain way—for example, as "a first-house person" or "first-house people," which simply means that someone has planets placed in that specific house in their birth chart. Some people have many planets in the same house. When someone has more than three planets placed in one sign or house, this is called a *stellium*. A stellium of planets in one sign or house makes that energy stronger and intensifies lessons in that area of life. There are other people who have empty houses, with no planets in them. Many clients ask me why their houses are empty; it simply means that at the time of birth, the planets were not in that area of the sky. It is not a bad thing to have empty houses in your birth chart.

When I talk about a *house cusp*, I will be referring to the specific sign that falls on that house on the birth wheel. For instance, if Virgo is your ascendant, that sign might fall on the twelfth and first house cusps. If the sun was placed on the cusp of the twelfth and first houses, it means the energy of both houses can affect your life, so make sure to read both descriptions.

MY OWN HEALING EXPERIENCE WITH ASTROLOGY

Now that we've covered the astrological basics, I want to explain why I think astrology and healing go hand in hand. Astrology helped me heal and gave me tools to understand myself better.

As a Virgo, I had always struggled with overthinking and shyness. Virgo is known as the worrier of the zodiac, and it's ruled by the planet Mercury, which controls thoughts and the mind. After understanding my Virgo sun sign personality traits better, I realized that my thoughts really affected my mood. I discovered how that could negatively impact my health. Writing and journaling have always balanced my thoughts and emotions, and realizing that Mercury rules Virgo helped me understand why.

Now, I try to incorporate writing into my daily self-care plan. I have healed many things by realizing that I can only control one thing: my own mind. I wanted to write this book to help readers understand their specific sun sign traits so they can use them to heal. I know that astrology can be a practical tool to help encourage healing and resiliency.

CHAPTER

ARIES & THE FIRST HOUSE

Nickname: Aries the Warrior

Symbol: The ram

Sun Sign Dates: March 21–April 19

Ruler: Mars

Rules: The first house; the head and face

Sign Type: Fire, cardinal

Polar Opposite Sign: Libra

Tips for Healing: Exercise, play sports, prioritize relaxation, practice anger management

A ries is a cardinal sign, which means Arians are initiators who enjoy creating new ideas and igniting change. They are naturally athletic, driven to achieve their goals, and highly competitive. They are ruled by the element of fire and are known to be passionate, energetic, charming, and charismatic. Because they appear restless, motivated, and friendly, others see Aries as a confident person who fights for what they believe in.

Being the first sign of the zodiac, Arians often get a bad reputation for being selfish and self-centered. The truth is that they are born self-reliant and have a strong desire to do things on their own. They dislike anything that restricts their ability to act; they always need to feel free to make decisions when feeling inspired. Taking action is a huge part of their personality, but acting too impulsively creates difficulties. Planning or thinking ahead is difficult for most Arians, and they don't always follow through from start to finish.

One of the hardest things for individuals to understand about Aries is that their spiritual mission is to be self-centered. It is no surprise that Aries rules the first house in the astrological chart, the house of the self. Arians express self-concern verbally and honestly.

CHALLENGING ATTRIBUTES OF AN ARIES

The natural ruler of Aries is the planet Mars, which increases feelings of impulsiveness, aggression, and passion. It's very difficult for an Aries to hold back because they feel everything in the moment, and they often lack the patience to think things through. One of the things Arians are known for is unleashing their powerful emotions in sharp and fast ways.

Arians can get a bad reputation for being brutally honest and extremely blunt. Speaking the truth is very important to them, and they want to surround themselves with people who are upfront and tell it like it is; this helps an Aries know where they stand with others because they value honesty above all else. But the intensity of how they express emotions such as anger can be hurtful to family and friends. This isn't personal; Arians are just focused on getting what they want using their laser-focused instincts. Nothing else matters to them when pursuing a goal, and they won't stop until they succeed (or lose interest). Because Arians never take time to think about how their actions will impact others, they sometimes leave a trail of hurt and angry people behind them, many of whom feel used, abused, or let down.

Pent-up anger and stress are common for Arians because they avoid contemplating their own problems. They tend to move on too quickly from experiences, pushing fiercely and aggressively toward the future. But avoiding dealing with problems often creates pain and emotional wounds that are left unhealed.

Issues involving commitment and relationship problems are some of the greatest challenges for Arians. They struggle to put other people's needs first because they are always looking out for number one: themselves. The primary reason for this behavior is that Aries rules the first house, which is the house of self, ego, identity, and independence. Primal survival instincts kick in that tell them to only depend on themselves, not on others.

Positive Attributes of an Aries
Passionate at heart, Arians have a desire to focus on pursuing their own emotions, urges, goals, and interests. They are always trying

to figure out ways to improve and elevate themselves through hard work and sheer determination. Because of this, they find it easy to move forward and try new things. As the initiator of the zodiac, Arians like to accomplish things first, and they utilize innovative ideas to obtain their goals.

At work, Arians are known to focus on the future by creating new ideas, projects, and goals for the outside world to admire. Life is a stage and a place where they can show off talents. Winning is very important and helps increase motivation. Arians are one of the most competitive and driven signs of the zodiac. They increase their self-esteem by excelling at various forms of competition; they like to be the best at everything they do. (Beware, though: sometimes Arians can hold a grudge. They find it difficult to admit that others might be just as good as them or better.)

Although they may appear selfish and arrogant, Arians are actually very loving and giving to those they care about. Egotistical behavior is not uncommon, but it is hard for loved ones to stay angry because they know Aries is capable of being a very affectionate, outgoing, and giving person. And even though Arians are known to have a temper and express their anger forcefully, it is also hard for them to stay angry at anyone for very long.

Sometimes it's important for an Aries to realize that not everyone is as brave, courageous, and forward-thinking as they are. As a true warrior who takes up their sword to fight any roadblock, challenge, or difficulty that comes their way, Aries never gives up. The energetic nature of an Aries is a strength that can be utilized when they are feeling depressed. These personality traits help an Aries overcome many obstacles, foster resilience, and conquer crisis and adversity.

Relationships with an Aries

Anyone who has had a relationship with an Aries understands that they do not like to be told what to do. Strong-willed, they like to act on their instincts and impulses in the moment and without hesitation. Sometimes these personality traits can cause difficulties in their relationships. Arians often experience communication problems and personality clashes with loved ones, family members, coworkers, and friends. If someone points out their flaws or negative behaviors, Aries are known to cut them off without notice and never speak to them again.

That famous temper can flare violently when an Aries feels controlled by others. When they feel threatened or exposed, a survival instinct kicks in telling them that freedom and independence are being hindered. Arians want to be self-reliant and hate to feel dependent on anyone. When Arians feel like they need others, they can get scared of that connection. They may push away those they love the most due to feeling too emotionally dependent on them. Those closest to Aries may accuse them of being uninterested and detached from day-to-day responsibilities.

One of the most sexual and passionate signs of the zodiac, Arians like a challenge and are affectionate in love. They are known for intense romantic feelings, simmering passions, and getting bored easily in relationships. Moving on from partners too quickly can be a problem.

Aries Tips for Transformation

Arians transform when they are able to freely move forward and express their desires in a healthy, balanced way. Embracing the fact that life is not always about survival and competition will help them bond with others. Transforming the self comes easily to an Aries, but shifting their focus to helping others can be more difficult. Learning to be patient with others is a major test for an Aries, but developing more patience and nurturing partnerships helps them accomplish great things.

Focus on Others

It might be difficult for an Aries to practice thinking about what others want and need. However, when they do this it helps transform self-centered traits that get in the way of achieving their goals. This is something Arians can work on and learn how to do with practice. Helping others achieve their goals and being a team player helps increase success. Arians need to practice balancing getting what they want at all costs with allowing others to get what they want as well. When an Aries can shift self-focused energy toward figuring out what others need, they will receive blessings.

Experience Romance

Romance transforms Aries because they enjoy the thrill of the chase. Emotional transformation comes through being in love and experiencing sexual intimacy. Being in love and expressing their romantic side in relationships makes them feel alive. Arians might want to try bungee jumping, skydiving, or hang gliding with their partner. Expressing their passionate spirit with those they love helps them transform stress, worry, and anxiety.

Overcome Self-Centeredness

Transformation comes through taking action and moving forward focused on the future instead of living in the past. Arians have an incredible ability to overcome challenging obstacles. When an Aries sets their mind to achieve something, they will stop at nothing to get it. However, taking others with them on that journey is important, and so is listening to the advice of loyal friends. Arians will grow stronger when they stop pushing other people away and allow others to help them.

ARIES TIPS FOR HEALING

An Aries experiences the greatest healing when they balance their need for total independence with interdependence. For an Aries to heal, they need strong relationships, but it is not easy for them to commit fully to another person, and this takes practice. Healing comes when an Aries learns to trust people and works on eliminating their selfish tendencies.

Find a Support System and Reduce Competitiveness

Arians need to have a sense of freedom, but they also need committed intimate relationships to heal many wounds. It is important for an Aries to learn that they don't have to do everything alone. Appearing weak is one of an Aries's greatest fears, but they need to avoid suffering in silence and overcome their fear of being vulnerable with others.

Arians often feel lonely because they feel like they can't truly depend on others in their life. Many have felt this way from a young age. As they grow older, Arians have to shift from focusing on themselves to nurturing relationships and building trust. Learning to bond with others by developing true partnerships that are based on friendship, loyalty, and compromise will help Arians achieve much more than they ever could on their own. This is one of the greatest lessons an Aries must learn.

Taking the time to allow others to support them instead of struggling alone during a crisis helps foster greater healing. It is important for an Aries to give themselves permission to trust that others have their back. It's also important for an Aries to learn that they can avoid competing with others. Once they realize that not everyone is competing with them, true healing can begin.

Control Anger

It is important for an Aries to practice controlling their anger and walking away from a frustrating situation. This helps them get a fresh perspective. If an Aries can take a deep breath, step away from whatever is upsetting them, and wait until they cool down, this will help prevent them from hurting people they care about. However, it's important for an Aries to speak their mind to a degree. If Arians bite their tongue, repress their desires, and avoid their feelings, they can eventually develop health problems. An Aries who avoids communicating with those they care about can burn out.

It is important for Arians to find a positive outlet for feelings of anger, aggression, and other powerful emotions. Exercise and physical activity are beneficial for Arians. Going for a run, punching a punching bag, or taking a kickboxing class can help release pent-up emotions. Finding new ways of expressing enormous amounts of physical energy will help balance an Aries's mind, body, and spirit. If physical activity does not work or if they don't have time to implement it in their daily life, then finding some other type of hobby will be beneficial. Spending time in nature, hiking, fishing, camping, and hunting might be things an Aries would enjoy.

Learn Patience

An Aries's impulsiveness can get them into trouble, which might cause feelings of regret or guilt. Arians must remember that the words they speak have an impact on others, so it's important to choose those words carefully.

When an Aries feels something strongly, they want to act immediately. They must practice slowing down and learn to take a deep breath before acting. Being forced to wait is something that will benefit them in the long run. Sometimes learning to wait can be a great challenge that needs to be overcome.

Aries can also heal by learning patience, because they won't always find solutions to problems as quickly as they'd like to. Learning to plan and consider future consequences will help them achieve much more than impulsive decisions ever will.

Process Difficult Emotions and Memories

It is important for an Aries to forgive themselves for the regrets of the past. Life is short. If Arians have made mistakes in the past, they can apologize and make amends to the people they hurt. If there are things an Aries avoids thinking about or feeling, they should allow themselves to feel them in order to heal. If there are things in the past that are holding an Aries back, it's important to make time to process them. The first step is acknowledging that they have wounds, which might be difficult for an Aries to admit. Appearing strong all the time can be draining, and there will be times when an Aries needs to admit they are not okay. Arians need to realize that allowing others to help and assist them is not a weakness, but a strength.

Manage Stress Effectively

When Arians don't manage stress effectively, it can manifest as physical illness. Aries rules the head, face, and brain, so an Aries's vulnerable area is the head, face, brain, cranium, and jaw. When they are experiencing mental stress, an Aries might suffer from headaches or migraines. Arians need to be careful when driving and operating machinery because they are prone to accidents or injuries to the head and face. Many Arians are born with underbites or overbites and experience problems with their jaw. When experiencing stress, they are known to grind and clench their teeth.

ARIES RESILIENCY

Arians are resilient because they have a warrior spirit. Warriors never give up; they continue to fight regardless of the outcome. Aries are strong, confident, and successful when they listen to that warrior voice within. Arians are blessed with a powerful strength and are self-motivated to face problems directly. And when an Aries feels free to choose and make their own decisions, they will feel even more resilient.

Another strength Arians possess is self-confidence. This helps them believe they can overcome any obstacle. This personality trait instinctively helps Aries overcome loss, pain, and betrayal. Survival instincts push an Aries forward to overcome anything life throws their way. Martian energy makes Arians naturally resilient. There is a fire inside of them that burns and pushes them forward. Arians are known to bounce back quickly from adversity and heartache. Leading the way and forging onward is their motto, as they rarely let anything get them down for long. Arians are born with a natural resiliency that can be utilized when they feel depressed, sad, angry, or alone.

Arians are excellent motivators and encourage those around them to believe in themselves. Extreme positivity can help an Aries overcome challenges during times of change. Using positive personality traits to help other people who are lost and unable to move forward will foster resiliency. Leading others into battle comes naturally for Aries. Their forte is convincing others that anything is possible, even when life seems difficult. It is also important for an Aries to take their own advice and learn to be their own cheerleader.

How to Support an Aries

If there is an Aries in your life, it's important to support their childlike nature and need for adventure. Give them the time to pursue their hobbies and interests. Recognize that routine kills their happiness; help them find new experiences and places to go together. Encourage them to be as independent and free as they need to be. Give them time alone, avoid controlling behaviors, and allow a lot of freedom, and an Aries will be happy.

Arians can be restless and find it hard to sit still, and they feel most comfortable when allowed to move freely. Encourage an Aries to create an exercise routine or have some other physical outlet to express their excessive energy; this can help combat feeling angry, irritated, or frustrated.

Aries Reflection Questions

- What helps you when you are angry?
- How can you learn to be more patient?

- Is there anything you need or want to heal?

- What personality traits help you become more resilient?

- How do you handle stress and anxiety?

ARIES AFFIRMATIONS

- "I am learning patience."

- "My Aries sun has given me the courage to be present with the trauma I have endured."

- "This tiny fire inside me pushes me forward when life knocks me down. Nothing will keep me down for long."

- "My passion and drive are my greatest strengths."

ARIES SELF-CARE IDEAS

- Be active. Make time for a workout routine. Try taking a martial arts class.

- Find a new hobby that is challenging and exciting.

- Join a sports team where you can compete and meet new people.

- Create three positive affirmations to recite daily.

- List three self-care techniques you find helpful and make time to do those things.

- Draw a flower with seven petals. Write down one new self-care activity you want to implement in each of the petals. Then hang the flower on the wall as a reminder. Try to do one new self-care activity every day until you've incorporated them into your routine.

THE FIRST HOUSE

The first house or ascendant starts the birth chart wheel, and it represents the personality that you show to the world. This energy is actually a mask that hides your true inner nature. The ascendant (or rising sign) is what I call the trickster. It can make others observe you a certain way, and they may misjudge your personality based on that. For instance, if the first house is in Leo, other people will perceive you as attractive, magnetic, composed, self-assured, and confident even if that is not your true nature.

The first house fully embodies all issues related to physical appearance. This is the house of the self and symbolizes areas such as body image, self-esteem, health concerns, and fashion preferences. Overall behaviors, mannerisms, and drives of a person are ruled by the first house.

If you don't have any planets in the first house, that is not a bad thing. It does not mean that you won't experience positive energy in that area of life. To gain greater insight, you will need to look at the sign that falls on the house cusp. For instance, when Virgo is on the first house cusp, you will appear shy, quiet, and analytical. You will be observant, and you will notice small things that others don't in the environment.

PLANETS IN THE FIRST HOUSE

I find when there is more than one planet in the first house, it creates a personality that is intense, passionate, and extremely magnetic. It is no surprise that the sign Aries rules the first house; this is why there is a powerful energy associated with this house. People who have planets here are strong, bold, straightforward, daring, confident, and independent spirits. First-house people are goal-oriented and find strength when faced with challenges.

People who have planets in their first house might have difficulty holding back thoughts and feelings. When there is more than one planet in the first house, this creates passionate and intense emotions. You often exude strength and possess a powerful energy that impacts the environment and those around you; this could be positive or negative. Other people are often extremely attracted to or repelled by your magnetic personality.

Being first and winning any battle is important to you. You might become obsessed with goals and desires to the extent that you forget others have dreams too. You shine when given the freedom to move and achieve your goals without restriction. Growth comes from experiencing autonomy, and this helps first-house people thrive. If you feel withheld or repressed, you can lash out at others in anger. You won't tolerate anyone standing in your way. You excel at sports or any type of competition where you can win. But you should be careful about competing with everyone in your life, because this can damage friendships, partnerships, and relationships.

You must learn that partnerships can be beneficial and overcome impatience when developing intimate relationships; these are lessons of the first house. Committing to others and compromising are strengths that can be developed. When planets are in the first house, the end goal is to become more aware of others and their needs.

You need constant adventure in your life as well as physical movement to balance stress. Playing sports, exercising, and physical fitness are crucial for emotional and physical health.

Involvement in games or sports helps encourage a positive expression of first-house energy. It's important for you to do things that make you feel alive and push you outside of your comfort zone.

If You Have Planets in the First House

If you have one or more planets in the first house, read the corresponding section for tips for transformation, healing, and resilience.

Sun in the First House

You are a person who puts great effort into maintaining a positive self-image. Sometimes changing your appearance helps you feel better. With the sun placed here, people see a happy and energetic person. Your personality impacts others and your surroundings in a positive way. Attracting positive people into your life comes naturally because of your enthusiasm and confidence. Always try to harness a positive outlook because this will help you overcome life's challenges.

Asserting yourself and speaking the truth boldly and honestly is one of your greatest strengths. Learning not to care what people think about you is one of your greatest challenges. Be careful about always wanting to be the center of attention. Learn to focus on the needs and wants of others; this will help balance self-centered tendencies.

Moon in the First House

You are a person whose emotions and feelings show on your face. People can easily see how you feel, which makes it hard to hide anything from others. Having physical security and emotional safety is important for you to feel comfortable. The environment impacts your emotions, so it is important to surround yourself with positive people.

When you act, you do so based on feelings because listening to your gut instinct helps you make better decisions. Be careful about behaving impulsively and on pure instinct. Sometimes it is helpful to wait and patiently think about situations.

Learning to nurture yourself and creating boundaries with others will help you find greater happiness. Using your emotional strength helps you overcome obstacles and challenges. When you are experiencing emotional crisis, protecting yourself comes naturally and helps you maintain stability.

Mercury in the First House
You are an intellectual person who likes to analyze the environment. Discussing your ideas and strong opinions with others helps you feel supported, but it is important to control your need to talk about yourself too much. When you learn to balance your thoughts, it helps counter stress and anxiety. Sometimes your mind is so active that you are already thinking about what you are going to say next, and you are known to interrupt other people when they are speaking. Writing and journaling can be a beneficial tool to express your restless energy. Learn patience by opening up to other people's ideas and work on active listening skills.

Venus in the First House
You are a person who is charming, magnetic, soft, and attractive. You are perceived as beautiful and elegant, and your personality impacts everyone. Be cautious about becoming a people pleaser and work on becoming comfortable with conflict. In love, make sure you attract healthy partners and avoid challenging people.

Be aware that toxic people and unpleasant situations can affect your health.

It is important to have a calm, peaceful, and stable environment to ensure happiness. Express your artistic talents by carving out time for creative pursuits. Focus on taking care of your physical body and appearance by pampering yourself with salon visits, massages, and facials.

Mars in the First House

You are a person who is straightforward, and people know you are driven. You are talented at being direct, abrupt, and assertive; you let people know what you believe and feel right away. Because you are an honest communicator, others always know where you stand.

Remember that life is not a battle to be won. Sometimes you feel you can't rely on others and try to do everything on your own. Partnering with others can help you achieve your goals faster. When you work on trusting others, your life will improve. Developing patience, taming your anger, and controlling selfishness will help you make more friends.

One of your greatest challenges is making sure to think before you act. Utilize your naturally competitive spirit, confidence, and self-reliance to overcome any obstacles in your path.

Jupiter in the First House

You are a person who has a happy and generous personality. Doing things that make a big impact and improve the lives of others is important to you. Positivity exudes from you, and others see you as a go-getter who can achieve anything. Overcoming challenges and unpleasant situations is easier for you than it is for others.

Being more realistic and practical and balancing your giving nature is a challenge. With this placement, make sure to remember that rules and boundaries are needed in life. Learn moderation when expressing your high energy level; this will help overcome burnout and frustration.

Saturn in the First House

You are a serious person who can appear sad or depressed. From an early age you have been mature, cautious, and aware of the realities of life. It is good to accept responsibilities, but don't let them limit your pursuit of happiness.

A lesson for this placement is to let go and release the need to control situations and people. It is critical to make time for fun and adventure. Schedule time to pursue your hobbies or any projects that bring you happiness. Practice expressing yourself without fear of others' approval or judgment. This placement causes inhibitions, so work on loosening rigid beliefs and focus on developing a more optimistic outlook. Remember to stop taking things so seriously and learn to relax. Increase your self-esteem, build greater self-confidence, and start believing in yourself!

Uranus in the First House

You are a person who appears aloof and detached from the environment. Expressing your identity in unique ways, such as dressing or acting differently than others, is how you get attention. You do not really care if you fit in and might like to shock people by being different. Creating innovative ways of accomplishing goals and thinking outside the box comes naturally to you.

Rebelling against authority figures and not caring what other people think about you is a lesson of Uranus in the first house.

This placement intellectualizes feelings, and this can cause difficulty when making decisions. If you can utilize your unique personality traits to embrace change, then you can overcome many challenges.

Neptune in the First House

You are a person who senses emotional undercurrents in the environment. Mysterious, dreamy, and spiritual, you use your compassionate spirit to help those less fortunate. It's second nature.

Learning to trust your intuition and acting on imaginative feelings will not lead you astray. This placement can make you secretive, so work on communicating openly with others. It is natural for you to want to withdraw from the environment, but learn to balance these feelings and work on participating in social activities.

Insecurities can get in the way and affect your ability to trust other people. Developing stronger boundaries will help you avoid feelings of being taken advantage of by those you care about. Developing a spiritual path and implementing it in a practical way will be beneficial for you.

Pluto in the First House

You are a person who has a powerful presence that impacts the environment. And if you learn to release your controlling behaviors, you can achieve much more. Learning to control passionate, intense, and unhealthy emotions such as anger, jealousy, and revenge will help encourage healing. Accepting that life has many endings and beginnings helps you grow as a person.

This placement creates a powerful energy that emanates around your physical body, and others perceive you as deep, secretive, and transformative. Born with a healing presence, you act as a catalyst of change in the lives of others. Because you are a natural counselor and therapist, other people approach you and share their problems with you. Your presence brings comfort, support, and renewal to those who have wounds.

Taurus & the Second House

Nickname: Taurus the Stabilizer

Symbol: The bull

Sun Sign Dates: April 20–May 20

Ruler: Venus

Rules: The second house; the throat, neck, and shoulders

Sign Type: Earth, fixed

Polar Opposite Sign: Scorpio

Tips for Healing: Spend time in nature, try relaxation techniques, enjoy in moderation

T aurus is a fixed sign, which means Taureans are strong-willed, determined, and stable. They do not like surprises or the unexpected. Feeling grounded makes them feel safe. Taurus is ruled by the element of earth, and earth signs are known for their practicality, work ethic, and need for structure. At first glance, others see them as easygoing, friendly, and charming—until they get to know them better. Then they quickly realize that Taureans are actually very stubborn and focused on material success. Taureans are extremely strong-willed individuals who know what they want. They like to do things their own way (which is sometimes the hard way) and think about each step before making decisions.

One of their greatest fears is making impulsive decisions when it comes to personal security and their future. Taureans want to be prepared for any challenge, but they need to realize that is an impossible goal because life is always changing. People change and emotions change, and sometimes a Taurus needs to adapt and follow the flow of energy. Things happen in life that are out of everyone's control. When the unexpected happens, Taureans can have difficulty accepting these new changes. It's important for a Taurus to learn to embrace change fully.

The most important thing for a Taurus to learn is to let go of things they can't change. Taureans are known to cling tightly to people they care about, situations they want to control, and material possessions they are connected to. Collecting things and accumulating possessions comes naturally, but accumulating too many material things can tie a Taurus down and cause feelings of being stuck. It is crucial to release old patterns of energy and embrace what is new in order to avoid stagnation. Releasing the past with forgiveness creates a lighter feeling in the body.

It is not surprising that the second house in a birth chart is ruled by Taurus. The second house is known as the house of money, financial security, self-worth, and emotional comfort. Money is important to Taureans, but not because of the power it has—they feel money and security go hand in hand. Anything that brings lasting security and stability is important, and they like to have control over material things. Taureans fear not having enough or going without, and this can affect their ability to find true happiness. They are constantly planning for the future, thinking about everything that could go wrong, and worrying about challenges that could come their way.

Taureans become stronger people when they put value on things that are not monetary or material. Doing things that benefit others strengthens their sense of self-esteem and self-worth. The more a Taurus allows themselves to trust others and the Universe, the more confident they will become. This will help them develop the ability to accept change without resisting it.

CHALLENGING ATTRIBUTES OF A TAURUS

Resisting change and becoming rigid in their beliefs—especially if others are forcing them to do something that they are unsure about—is common. An inability to move forward due to fear or feeling unprepared can hold them back. They can be coaxed into making small changes if they respect the person trying to help them. It takes a special person to convince a Taurus that it is safe to step out of their comfort zone. They need friends who can speak in a way that relieves insecurities and anxieties.

If a Taurus feels abused or forced to change, strong emotions and a hidden temper can ignite. Taureans are usually slow to anger, but when they feel trapped other people are often shocked to see how upset they can become. In general, Taureans dislike showing negative emotions and try to be peaceful, pleasant, and easygoing. When they do experience stress, this is typically when others see them express strong emotions.

Practical and diligent, Taureans find it hard to change their beliefs, values, behaviors, and life path. They are perceived as rigid and inflexible because once they make up their mind, very few people can change it.

Positive Attributes of a Taurus

One of the most patient signs of the zodiac, Taureans are able to wait, plan, analyze, and make things happen slowly. They are excellent at planning and preparing financially for the unknown; this is one of their greatest strengths. Some people might feel they are lazy or lack initiative because they appear laid-back and carefree.

Born with a strong sense of morality and a passion for traditional religion, doing the right thing is important for a Taurus. They are often interested in traveling, higher education, and studying foreign cultures. Success comes through pursuing careers in finance, business, teaching, or even ministry. Taureans are hardworking, predictable, reliable, and extremely resourceful. When they put their mind to something, they will not stop until they achieve it. Nothing can sway them from goals, even though it might take much longer to reach them than other signs.

Since Taurus is ruled by the planet Venus, Taureans are known to possess creative and artistic abilities. Excelling in the performing arts is common, and many Taureans are known to have a beautiful singing voice. They might enjoy painting, drawing, or making things with their hands such as pottery and jewelry. Listening to music benefits Taureans because it helps soothe the soul and also helps reduce stress.

Comfort and security are crucial for a Taurus's emotional well-being. Taureans find security in peaceful surroundings. There is nothing more healing for them than enjoying a good meal, wine, and a romantic dinner with someone they love. Having beautiful art and material things surrounding them in their home makes them feel comfortable. Because they are so in touch with their senses, they can be particular about certain things in the environment. Taureans also have high standards and specific likes and dislikes when it comes to food, music, and decorations.

It's common for Taureans to have allergies or sensitivities to light, sounds, textures, or smells. Having soft blankets to snuggle with, comfortable clothes to wear, and flowery essential oils to diffuse brings healing.

RELATIONSHIPS WITH A TAURUS

Taureans are notorious for asking for advice and seeking other people's opinions, but they don't always listen to others or implement their advice. Strong-willed and stubborn at heart, they often think they know best. Problems come up in relationships due to their inability to trust others fully because they often believe they are right. Sometimes those closest to a Taurus feel like they steer away from communication to avoid arguments. Taureans are natural peacemakers and will do anything to avoid conflict.

Taureans like making their own decisions because they don't like the feeling of being rushed. More spontaneous individuals can create irritation because winging things and taking risks is scary for a Taurus. Sometimes others feel they wait too long, often avoiding decision-making, and miss out on important opportunities. Friends and family can become impatient with a Taurus because it may seem like they are never going to make a firm decision. It's important for others to understand that Taureans are trying to think ahead and prepare for everything that might go wrong.

Taurus is one of the most affectionate signs of the zodiac. Taureans need physical affection and enjoy cuddling with those they love. Being ruled by Venus intensifies the individual's senses, especially physical touch. Taureans are known to be sensual, and touch helps them reduce stress. They crave comfort and feeling cozy, so there is nothing better than snuggling with friends, family, and pets.

Sometimes when a Taurus clings to things too long, the Universe forces things to be stripped away unexpectedly. Cutting off attachments that are outdated or unhealthy will bring greater healing because a Taurus's greatest growth happens when they embrace the unexpected and let go. However, the process of loss can be intensely painful and more difficult for Taureans. Be patient and recognize that healing the past can take time and effort.

TAURUS TIPS FOR TRANSFORMATION

Taureans will transform when they are able to listen to others' advice. Sometimes they have a hard time accepting or believing what others say.

Find Self-Worth

Feeling rushed to make decisions makes it harder for a Taurus to take action. They are known to be quiet and hide unless they feel comfortable and safe. Because of this, Taureans do not always stand up for themselves. Repressing unpleasant emotions causes difficulties, but this behavior can be transformed when they learn to express emotions in healthy ways.

Taureans may struggle to move forward in life after the unexpected happens. They benefit by learning how to communicate hurt feelings on the spot. If they wait and hold back in the moment, they often regret it.

One of the most important lessons for a Taurus to learn is that they shouldn't dwell on situations that can't be controlled. They also need to learn to accept that their ideas are just as good as others'. Taurus needs to accept that they are worthy of love and deserve good things in life, which will bring greater self-worth.

Listen to Others

It's isolating when a Taurus shuts other people out and refuses to discuss their problems with others. Suffering in silence is unhealthy and causes anxiety, sadness, and other health problems. Opening up and sharing their emotions with loved ones will help a Taurus reduce stress.

Taureans have strong opinions, beliefs, and thoughts. They can transform their relationships with others when they actively listen to what people are saying, consider it, and incorporate others' ideas into their life. Doing this will help a Taurus gain the respect of others.

Remembering that they do not have to do everything on their own is key to finding happiness. If a Taurus allows others to help, they will feel a weight lifted off their shoulders and heavy burdens will be released. When a Taurus works with others and compromises, they can achieve much more in life.

Allow Change

Sometimes Taureans struggle to let go of their need to control the outcome of situations. Accepting change creates more growth, makes a Taurus stronger, and attracts positive relationships.

Taureans often stay rooted in where they are instead of embracing where they could be due to a lack of confidence in some areas of life. Embracing change helps a Taurus realize new energy can be motivating while attracting more success. Remembering that they are human and can't predict every obstacle in life can help them find inner strength.

Balance Finances

Taureans should have an easier time than most signs with saving money and preparing for the future. Because they are focused on financial matters, this ensures their family will be taken care of. As a lover of nice things, Taureans will find comfort in owning a home, having land, and preparing for retirement. However, transforming the way they spend money and their attitude toward finances is critical in balancing fears of failure.

Taureans are notorious for being thrifty and often avoid spending money on anything they feel is impractical. A Taurus's greatest strength is their ability to focus on needs versus wants, but being very practical can be a burden at times. Taureans tend to focus on the physical pillar and ensure all basic needs are met, such as housing, food, and clothing. This is noble as long as emotional needs are also nourished. We all like to have money in the bank for a rainy day, but Taureans shouldn't forget to live and enjoy life. This behavior can create a feeling of deprivation and affect happiness or cause difficulties in relationships. It is important to find middle ground; Taureans need flexibility for saving but should also allow spending.

Transformation occurs when Taurus steps out of their comfort zone and allows themselves to splurge once in a while. If spending money stresses them out, they should slowly start to spend it on things they normally would not purchase to get used to these feelings. Using an inborn strength and determination helps push Taurus toward overcoming all of life's challenges.

TAURUS TIPS FOR HEALING

Taureans heal by overcoming stubbornness. Learning to adapt and listen to the thoughts and ideas of others strengthens the healing process. In order to heal personal relationships, it's important to learn to compromise and allow forgiveness. Accepting that they can be wrong—and admitting it!—helps reduce conflict with others. Taureans can make an extra effort by asking loved ones what they think, feel, and believe.

Overcome Stubbornness

Taureans heal by being less rigid, stubborn, and close-minded. It's important for Taureans to learn to take action and avoid waiting too long or they might miss out on great opportunities. Their preconceived notions about how things should be can block communication with others and make others withdraw. Many struggles Taureans face in life are related to resisting change and not listening to the advice of others.

Take Action

To heal, Taureans need to take action and avoid getting stuck in their own head. Sometimes a Taurus feels incapable of taking action due to overthinking or irrational fears. Holding on to the way they have always done things helps encourage a need for control. But doing things the same way every time blocks growth, so learning to snap out of routines and spice things up can bring relief.

No one can ever be fully prepared for unexpected change because its purpose is to ignite growth. Taureans heal by embracing this truth and welcoming it with open arms. When they take action, they will attract more of what they want and release old baggage. Healing comes when they get out of their comfort zone, take some risks, and see what it feels like to step forward with faith.

Let Go of the Past

Healing happens for Taureans when they allow themselves to let go of the past. This requires releasing relationships, beliefs, and emotions that might have caused pain. Healing cannot enter a Taurus's life until they stop repressing painful emotions and past memories.

Suppressing feelings can have a negative effect on the body and mind. When Taureans recognize the weight that will be lifted off their shoulders once they let go of past worries and negative thoughts and experiences, true healing and growth can happen in their lives.

Taureans have to take care of themselves by cutting ties with the past once and for all. They like to reminisce about the good old days and hold on to fond memories of being a child. They are connected to the past, but it can have a vice grip on life to the point of making them incapable of moving forward. The present moment is the only place where Taureans can truly heal. When they are struggling, it is important for a Taurus to remember that time heals all wounds.

Practice Self-Care

For Taurus, physical illness manifests in the weakest areas of their body, which are the neck, shoulders, and throat. Many suffer from thyroid disease or hormonal imbalances. When they are experiencing stress, it manifests as muscle pain, tension, and spasms in the neck or shoulders. Making time to get a massage or visit a chiropractor is beneficial to help release built-up tension. Taureans are also prone to ear infections, tonsillitis, laryngitis, and weight gain. Losing weight might be difficult to achieve due to stress eating because food brings comfort and relieves unpleasant emotions temporarily.

It's common for Taureans to have unhealthy coping methods involving food, such as overeating when they are stressed. Taureans need to be cautious about overindulging in desserts and sweets. Developing unhealthy habits that soothe them in the moment should be avoided in the long run because they may cause health problems. Addressing these issues head on helps heal issues surrounding comfort. Creating healthy eating and sleeping habits to counter stress will help a Taurus recharge.

TAURUS RESILIENCY

Taureans are resilient because they have a patient strength. They can overcome many obstacles because of their strong will and desire to achieve goals. Strong and sturdy, they should use their trait of unbeatable patience to overcome all obstacles. As the bull, they put their horns down and charge forward, not afraid of whatever is standing in their way.

A Taurus's resiliency is tied to their wholehearted belief in their dreams and goals. They possess the strength to survive difficult times in practical ways, which helps them bounce back from disappointment. It might take a Taurus a little more time to rise up again after they experience loss and challenges, but growth occurs when they learn to release the things they can't control. Accepting that the past is in the past makes Taurus stronger. Resilience happens when they are able to make small changes day by day.

Preparing for the unknown will help Taureans overcome unexpected life experiences. Planning, organizing, and saving money can protect Taurus when tragedy strikes. Taureans are the most prepared sign in the zodiac due to formidable willpower and planning abilities. They stubbornly push forward in life, slowly and deliberately. These personality traits assist them in difficult times and help them overcome emotional pain. Learning to utilize their natural patience helps a Taurus overcome and adapt to the unexpected.

How to Support a Taurus

If there is a Taurus in your life, support them in achieving their goals. Respect their need for personal space. Accept their strong values and beliefs. Don't push them to change if they are not ready. Spoil them with a lot of physical affection. Be committed and loyal. Cook for them and give them a massage. Be patient when they don't want to make a decision. Encourage them to incorporate change into their life.

TAURUS REFLECTION QUESTIONS

- What helps you when you feel stuck?
- How can you learn to embrace change?
- Is there anything you need or want to heal?
- What personality traits help you become more resilient?
- How do you handle stress and anxiety?

TAURUS AFFIRMATIONS

- "I heal by being in nature. I need time to reflect and to let my mind wander."
- "Being in my own home and nesting is very therapeutic for me. I need my alone time."
- "I am strong and push through any challenges like a bull."
- "Forgiveness is something I need to give to myself and others."

TAURUS SELF-CARE IDEAS

- Spend time outdoors, gardening and enjoying nature.
- Schedule a nice neck and shoulder massage with a professional.
- Listen to soothing music, express your creative side, and cook your favorite meal.
- Create three positive affirmations to recite daily.

- List three self-care techniques you find helpful and make time to do those things.

- Draw a flower with seven petals. Write down one new self-care activity you want to implement in each of the petals. Then hang the flower on the wall as a reminder. Try to do one new self-care activity every day until you've incorporated them into your routine.

THE SECOND HOUSE

Human beings enjoy security and are not always comfortable with change. We like to plan for our future and set goals for ourselves. Many of us enjoy having money and believe that having financial success will somehow make everything right in our lives. The second house in a birth chart is the house of finances, security, comfort, and self-worth. It represents what you truly value in life, both monetarily and emotionally. The second house also shows where you can find financial success and the creative ways you can make money and accumulate possessions. Having difficulty letting go of possessions, the past, emotions, and people are all second-house issues. It is no surprise that the sign Taurus rules this house, as most Taureans do not enjoy change and resist letting go of things. Besides finding financial security and enjoying the comforts of the world such as food, clothing, and art, the second house is also relevant in an individual's search for a sense of self-worth. Learning what is worthy and valuable as well as learning what money cannot buy are important lessons of this house.

Your personal karma with finances, property, and money is associated with the second house. Depending on which planets are placed in the second house, you may be the type of person that attracts money easily (like if Jupiter is placed there). If your karma is difficult—for example, if Saturn is in the second house—this can leave you feeling like you never have enough to feel secure.

If you don't have any planets in the second house, this simply means that the house issues will not be paramount in your life. Remember to look at the sign on the house cusp to analyze what energy impacts that area of life. For instance, if Aquarius is on the second house cusp, there is often a desire to own unique, creative, and eccentric material items. You might make money in unexpected ways, or your financial situation might go through ups and downs. There is also a strong need to express your values and to be recognized for being different than others.

IF YOU HAVE PLANETS IN THE SECOND HOUSE

When planets are placed in the second house, you enjoy security. Second-house people desire having money in the bank and financial security from owning land and property. This house represents what you truly value in life, and it especially teaches you to value yourself. Monetary changes and emotional needs are key issues you have to deal with.

Planets in the second house create a determined, strong-willed person and push you to continue working hard for what you want. These personality traits help create success in many areas of life. Working hard comes naturally to you, and you might work long hours to attain your goals. Planets here make you an excellent employee and coworker because you are driven to succeed. Second-house people are known to slowly take steps toward the finish line after much hard work, long hours, and unyielding determination. Planning for the future and setting goals makes it easier for you to achieve your dreams. You might worry about retirement from a young age. Possessions are an important part of your life, and you are focused on building a nest egg for the future. There might be a need to restrict yourself from obtaining things you truly want due to fears of the future.

When planets are in the second house, you tend to doubt yourself and second-guess things; you would rather stay in an unpleasant situation than make any small changes. Craving a routine where things are done the same way every time is a second-house trait. Remembering that life is full of change and a normal routine is not always possible can help second-house people adapt to change. You grow when you relinquish the need to control everything. When you learn to embrace change with ease and flow with new energy, you are better able to receive blessings from the Universe.

Relationships are an area of difficulty for second-house people. Avoiding making changes in your personal life can result in relationship problems. Holding on too tightly and not letting go even when things are causing pain is not beneficial. This behavior can be a trap for second-house people; you may be stuck in unpleasant situations longer than you should be. Even when you are miserable or suffering emotionally, you often stay in situations, relationships, or jobs because of your innate fear of the unknown. You need an environment that feels safe, secure, warm, and comfortable. Organize your world into a comfortable safe haven and allow greater emotional security by doing things that nurture your values.

It is important to address issues surrounding self-esteem when planets are located in the second house. Learning to accept and heal insecurities will help you develop the strength to take action during crisis. An important life lesson for second-house people is to learn to love yourself. Developing a sense of self-worth is paramount to inner happiness and the ability to love others. You are special and your ideas are important. Accumulating all the money and material possessions in the world does not always bring contentment or happiness.

PLANETS IN THE SECOND HOUSE

If you have one or more planets in the second house, read the corresponding section for tips for transformation, healing, and resilience.

Sun in the Second House

You express your main identity by sharing your personal values and accumulating material things. Figuring out what you want and taking action to obtain it should be your focus. With that being said, it's important to value the opinions of others and to listen to those you care about. Don't let stubbornness and an inflexible attitude affect your relationships.

Use your talents and financial resources to seek opportunities that create stability and purpose. Learning to believe in your own abilities will increase self-esteem. Express yourself by pursuing future goals. Live your best life by embracing comfort, stability, and advice from others.

Moon in the Second House

You are a person who focuses on finding emotional comfort and peace. Accept the fact that emotions will fluctuate, and this placement creates many ups and downs. It is also important to let go of past wounds surrounding self-worth, which will foster greater healing.

Having money in the bank and owning possessions bring you stability and comfort. Achieving material success comes with this placement, but sometimes there are difficulties enjoying it. It's important to learn to control your emotional fears and worries about not having enough. Learn to overcome your thrifty nature by being more giving. Working in the garden and being outdoors can nurture your soul. The moon in the second house craves anything that brings comfort such as wine, food, music, or art.

Mercury in the Second House

You are a person who spends most of their time thinking about financial security. It is also important to spend time thinking about what is important and valuable. Making the right connections comes naturally to you because you have a gift for partnering with successful people and communicating ideas with them. To snap out of boring routines, you like to shake things up. Flexibility and adaptability are heightened with this placement, which helps balance out second-house energy. Highly efficient, this placement helps you accomplish large amounts of work because of an ability to multitask.

Venus in the Second House

You are a person who will find pleasure in the material world. You are happiest when you are comfortable, safe, and surrounded by beautiful possessions. Born with specific tastes concerning clothes, foods, and possessions, it is important for you to enjoy the finer things in life.

This placement easily attracts abundance. Making money can come easily with this placement, but be cautious about wasting money on frivolous things.

Learning to let go of past relationships and old feelings can be challenging for you. Building relationships should be a key part of your life. Practice showing affection to others and expressing your artistic talents.

Mars in the Second House

You are a person who has strong desires, wants, and needs. Forcefully pursuing material possessions is the primary energy of this placement. Mars in the second house is focused on personal goals, and strength comes from transforming self-esteem and increasing self-worth. Taking risks with money and finances brings the excitement and challenges you crave. Excessive desires, needs, and impulsive spending habits need to be balanced.

With this placement, anger ignites quickly, especially when facing loss or stressful circumstances. With sheer determination, Mars in the second house is always in pursuit of owning things. Driven to succeed, working hard to achieve financial security comes naturally. This placement creates a person who stops at nothing to achieve their goals. Just be careful not to be selfish in these pursuits.

Jupiter in the Second House

You are a person who has a positive outlook and believes that everything will work out in life. Seeing the good in others attracts positive experiences and relationships. Sunny, positive, and optimistic, you have a natural faith that everything will be taken care of in the future. Even if you don't focus on material gain, this placement indicates good fortune and abundance. Spending money and making money come easily to you, and you have good luck in financial matters.

Since you always seem to have what you need, be careful with overindulgence. Embrace the law of giving and receiving, which will help increase wealth. Because you are extremely generous, taking care of others financially and giving expensive gifts is something that brings joy.

Saturn in the Second House

You are a person who feels restricted and burdened by financial responsibilities. There might be a feeling of lack or fear of never having what you need. Surviving in the world and maintaining a practical financial situation are always on the forefront of your mind. The burden of having to pay bills and worry about the future can cause depression and resentment. Possessions and family responsibilities can make you feel trapped.

Because you were born with a conservative and restrictive nature, it is important to learn to have more fun. Transform your cautious nature by being more generous. It is important to release controlling behaviors and to embrace change. Releasing the past can help heal karmic wounds related to self-worth.

Uranus in the Second House

You are a person who will experience sudden and unexpected changes in financial status. Feeling financially free is important with this placement; owning unique possessions and having eccentric tastes is common. Living a practical life is frustrating because you dislike following rules, paying bills, owning a home, or worrying about money. You tend to detach from the mundane responsibilities of the world because tedious tasks can cause feelings of restriction.

Financial matters can have many highs and lows, making it hard to ever feel grounded and emotionally secure. You may earn money in unexpected ways, like through hobbies or an inheritance. Listening to flashes of insight and brilliant ideas helps transform your self-esteem issues.

Neptune in the Second House

You are a person who enjoys making money utilizing your artistic talents. Responsibilities can seem overwhelming; you may want to escape reality with this placement. You may ignore material possessions because you don't value them as much as spiritual ideas and beliefs. Meaningful things such as spirituality, art, and expressing creativity are ways to find greater self-worth and conquer disillusionment. Learn to balance your imagination by living in the real world and seeing things clearly.

If you focus on finding happiness through work, you can avoid feeling burdened by living in the practical world. This placement brings good luck when making money, doing spiritual work, or helping those who suffer. Managing material responsibilities and becoming more practical is a lesson with Neptune in the second house.

Pluto in the Second House

You are a person who experiences intense feelings about making money and accumulating possessions. There is a powerful need to have material possessions and control over finances. This placement brings dramatic changes to your income and financial security. Cycling through periods of gaining material items and then losing them is common. Feeling secure can be difficult with this placement, and there are often unsettling feelings surrounding loss. Anticipating change that could affect your sense of comfort and security helps you prepare for the unexpected. Believe that you have the strength to start over and rebuild after times of adversity. As a natural healer, you have powerful regenerative abilities, a deep sense of self-worth, and an inborn intuition that guides your decisions.

CHAPTER

GEMINI &
THE THIRD HOUSE

Nickname: Gemini the Communicator

Symbol: The twins

Sun Sign Dates: May 21–June 21

Ruler: Mercury

Rules: The third house; the hands and lungs

Sign Type: Air, mutable

Polar Opposite Sign: Sagittarius

Tips for Healing: Slow down, learn new things,
seek out mental challenges

Gemini is a mutable sign, which means Geminis are easy-going, adaptable, and changeable. Often changing direction without notice, they are one of the most restless signs of the zodiac and have a hard time sitting still. Changing their mind often affects their behaviors and actions, sometimes frustrating others. As an air sign, Geminis are known to be emotionally aloof, intelligent, and excellent at communication. Geminis are known to be one of the friendliest zodiac signs. At first glance, they often mislead others due to their chameleon-like ways as they adapt to please those around them.

While they are not naturally athletic, making time to work out and participate in physical activity can help Geminis manage stress. It is very hard for a Gemini to meditate or still the mind, which can make it difficult to relax. Learning patience and developing mindfulness can help discipline the mind. Journaling, talking with close friends about problems, and reading books are all beneficial.

Challenging Attributes of a Gemini

One of the reasons Geminis have difficulty making decisions is because they are overthinkers. They can be indecisive and unreliable, and it can be hard for a Gemini to commit to things. Agreeing to do something in the moment often feels right, but later (when something more exciting happens), a Gemini's attention shifts and wanders.

Sometimes Geminis receive a bad reputation for hurting others. When they are feeling depressed or sad, lashing out at others verbally becomes a pattern of theirs. The comments they make can become sarcastic, cutting, and condescending. The person on the other end will either verbally strike back to defend themselves or be so dumbfounded that they retreat. Those who are tolerant will realize this behavior happens when Geminis are in a bad mood—and their mood fluctuates often.

POSITIVE ATTRIBUTES OF A GEMINI

Geminis are easy to connect with. They are social butterflies who enjoy communicating ideas and finding out what makes other people tick. Because they are extremely talkative, one of their greatest strengths is socializing and connecting with others. Geminis are ruled by the planet Mercury, which blesses them with a gift for words and expressing their thoughts and ideas.

Being ruled by Mercury also enhances the need to share information and express the self through writing and speaking, which makes Geminis excellent teachers. Learning new things, debating many different topics, and challenging people's ideas makes a Gemini feel alive.

Adaptable and flexible, Geminis can mimic the energy of those around them. They may even adapt their personality to match those they are interacting with. If someone is serious, Geminis will become serious. If someone is fun, then Geminis radiate fun. Gemini's famous trait is being able to charm others, and it is a natural gift.

RELATIONSHIPS WITH A GEMINI

Maintaining independence is important for Geminis, and they do not want to be tied down. They want to be able to leave in a moment's notice if they need to. In romantic relationships, Geminis tend to experience difficulties because they simply see good qualities in too many different people. The duality of this sign and the need for variety in all areas of life can cause struggles with commitment. From a young age they decided that monotony is boring. Because Geminis seek excitement and mental stimulation, they are known to wander off when a relationship grows stale, never to be seen again. The greatest test for a Gemini is to practice being in a committed partnership. Many Geminis decide to remain single and never marry by choice.

Flirtatious by nature, Geminis have many friends and connections with people from all walks of life. They love the social scene, partying in groups, having fun, and interacting with new people; all of this helps balance their high-strung behaviors. Geminis enjoy meeting new people, visiting new places, and eating at new restaurants. Experiencing constant "newness" in life brings a Gemini contentment.

Geminis love to share their feelings and struggle when they are held back from expressing themselves freely. They excel at communicating their deepest, darkest secrets with those they can trust. The only downside of talking so much is that it is hard for them to keep secrets, and repeating other people's secrets hurts others and causes distrust. It happens out of pure innocence on Gemini's part—they love to gossip and spread information, and once in a while they forget that some information should remain private.

Gemini Tips for Transformation

Geminis transform when they find time to slow down. Controlling how much energy they give to others will help prevent burnout.

Balance Your Energy

If they can learn to focus energy on one or two projects at a time instead of juggling multiple things, Geminis will become more efficient. Geminis are the twins, so they are known to do two things at once and see both sides of an issue, but problems arise when they have a full plate. Sometimes they struggle to finish projects and leave several things half done as they move forward too quickly to the next exciting idea. Learning to conserve their restless energy and focus it on what is important helps balance many areas of life.

Control Your Thoughts

Geminis can transform by focusing their mind and thoughts on positive things. Steering clear of negativity and avoiding worry will help reduce anxiety. When they control restless thoughts, they will be able to reduce stress levels and improve overall health. And if Geminis can find time to relax and ground their energy, then they will be capable of accomplishing incredible things.

Being ruled by the planet Mercury means that the mind can be a great strength or become a weakness. Geminis must be careful not to act irrationally and impulsively; they can counteract this tendency by remaining grounded. Being reliable and proving to others that they are trustworthy will help transform relationships.

The root of a Gemini's unstable behavior stems from the mind. If they practice meditation, focused mindfulness exercises, or breathing exercises, it will help stabilize their thoughts and emotions. Transformation begins when they learn how to control the enormous amount of physical and mental energy they possess.

Learn New Things

It is crucial for Geminis to spend time learning new things. They should stay busy and pursue hobbies and interests. Learning a new skill is beneficial as long as the skill enables them to work with their hands; they could learn to play an instrument, sew, or program computers.

Creative, rebellious, and adaptable, Gemini easily adapts to change and grows as an individual when they find time to unwind and be still. When they make time to study, read, and research new topics of interest, their energy will continue to balance out. Transformation comes by quenching their thirst for constant knowledge and exploration.

GEMINI TIPS FOR HEALING

There is a sense of instability that surrounds a Gemini, which makes it hard for others to trust what they say. They are known to have two very different sides to their personalities because they are the twins of the zodiac. Healing can come by accepting these two different personalities, no matter how different they may be.

Communicate Your Feelings

Gemini's biggest talent is processing information and making it available to others in some way. They often feel that others are not on their level mentally, which makes them feel lonely. Sometimes, even when surrounded by close friends, Geminis feel others can't keep up with their ideas and witty sense of humor. Learning to communicate their feelings and surrounding themselves with people who inspire them helps counter uncomfortable feelings like depression and isolation. Communication is important for a Gemini, and they need people who will listen.

With that being said, overcoming loneliness is a lesson Geminis must learn.

Geminis can truly heal when they accept that other people may never fully understand them or be able to keep up with them intellectually. Healing also comes by accepting romantic attractions not bound by sex, gender, race, or ethnicity. Geminis are attracted to many different types of people, and they like variety in relationships. Attraction starts on the mental plane for Geminis, and physical intimacy is not as important. They often fall in love with people who started off as friends.

Extroverted by nature, socializing with others is crucial for a Gemini's overall happiness. Sometimes communicating superficially on the surface level is more comfortable for a Gemini, but sharing deeper feelings with others fosters healing. Certain behaviors can cause difficulties connecting with others they care about. One of the highest risk factors for divorces or breakups is a lack of communication between partners. In friendships, Geminis find it easy to communicate, but in romantic relationships, it's difficult for them to communicate vulnerable feelings. Allowing themselves to be honest, open, and intimate with others is the key.

Overcome Boredom
Overcoming boredom helps a Gemini, but it's important to first figure out the deeper reasons why they are feeling bored in the first place. Analyzing themselves and developing greater self-awareness helps overcome moments of boredom. Geminis often feel they are lacking mental stimulation and a deep connection with other people. Other people often feel that Geminis are changeable and inconsistent.

Seeking constant excitement and stimulation can cause relationship problems. Geminis can heal relationships by communicating their feelings with others in an honest way. Sometimes they need to embrace the mundane, practical parts of life. Relationships bring challenges for Geminis, and if they can't connect mentally with someone, then they quickly move on. But healing the desire to move on too quickly from people that care about them is needed, because often Geminis regret losing them down the road.

Practice Mindfulness

Geminis are known for overthinking and replaying thoughts and scenarios in their head. They often experience nervous energy, which creates anxiety that can manifest as panic attacks or social anxiety. Finding things that help reduce their stress levels will be beneficial. If they take small steps toward being present in their body and centering themselves, they will feel better mentally, physically, and emotionally. Journaling and writing all their thoughts and emotions down on a piece of paper can help expunge unproductive thoughts by releasing them out of the physical body. Enjoying outdoor activities like Tai Chi and yoga can also help reduce anxiety and stress. Practicing stillness, mindfulness, and being present will accelerate Geminis' healing when they implement these things into their daily routine.

Geminis' vulnerable areas are the lungs, hands, arms, and nervous system, so strengthening their lungs by practicing breathing exercises is also an act of self-care. Geminis often suffer from allergies and colds, and they are prone to developing bronchitis and pneumonia.

Gemini Resiliency

Geminis are mental warriors. Geminis have an amazing mind. Mentally, no other sign can compete with them. They have a high vibration and stamina that pushes them toward their goals. When struggling with challenges in life, a Gemini is emotionally flexible, which helps them move on easily from challenges.

While other signs might take longer to bounce back after a crisis, Geminis thrive on constant change and growth. Experiencing crises can be exciting and can light a fire in their soul as they think about how to overcome. Thinking through challenges helps Geminis develop resilience and the patience to overcome adversity.

Born with an internal drive to move, adapt, change, and embrace the unexpected, Geminis spring back after tragedy strikes. Nothing really keeps a Gemini down for long. If they feel depressed or sad, they can use logic to overcome it. Finding ways to use their sense of humor is a strength that can help when things feel overwhelming. Geminis often keep their mind off their problems by distracting themselves. Being physically active and moving around can bring strength and resiliency. Because of their mutable, adaptable nature, Geminis are blessed with an ability to not get too wrapped up in emotion. Geminis are also good at helping others overcome their difficulties by giving them advice.

How to Support a Gemini

If there is a Gemini in your life, allow them to talk and listen to them. Stimulate their mind by discussing topics that are interesting. Don't shy away from deep conversations. Try to make them laugh. Share what you are thinking and feeling and ask them for help. When you notice that they are bored, find excitement together. Allow spontaneity, but also give them freedom to explore. Encourage them to pursue solitary activities.

Gemini Reflection Questions

- What helps you when you have restless thoughts?
- How can you learn to take time to relax and slow down?
- Is there anything you need or want to heal?
- How do you handle stress and anxiety?
- What personality traits help you become more resilient?

Gemini Affirmations

- "I am a good communicator and have healthy, loving relationships."
- "My greatest strength is my ability to bounce back after every ordeal."
- "I am heard and understood."
- "I heal by being active and spending time outdoors."

Gemini Self-Care Ideas

- Spend time playing games, doing puzzles, and socializing with close friends.
- Do something mentally challenging.
- Join a group or club so you can meet others who share similar interests.
- Create three positive affirmations to recite daily.

- List three self-care techniques you find helpful and make time do those things.

- Draw a flower with seven petals. Write down one new self-care activity you want to implement in each of the petals. Then hang the flower on the wall as a reminder. Try to do one new self-care activity every day until you've incorporated them into your routine.

THE THIRD HOUSE

As human beings, we thrive by communicating with each other. Without communication and social interaction with others, we can become depressed and withdrawn. The third house plays an important role in how we think and express ourselves. The ability to communicate with others—whether it is through the written word, verbally, or technologically via cell phones and computers—falls under the third house.

The third house is ruled by Gemini, the communicator and educator of the zodiac. Taking short journeys and traveling from place to place are third-house territory. When planets fall in the third house, this usually leads to increased intelligence in that area and, depending on the planet, there is an increased ability to remember and recall information.

If you don't have planets in the third house, it's important to look at the sign on the cusp of the house to see what energy impacts this area of life. For instance, if Scorpio is on the third house cusp, you might be secretive and private. You likely do not readily communicate with others. You have a tendency to hide your thoughts and feelings, and you dislike feeling vulnerable.

Communication needs to be deep and meaningful. Any superficial small talk will irritate you.

IF YOU HAVE PLANETS IN THE THIRD HOUSE

Third-house people are communicative, intellectual, nervous, versatile, sociable, sarcastic, and restless. Pursuing stimulating intellectual pursuits such as reading, writing, and teaching help stimulate the mind. Travel, communication, and basic knowledge are all related to this house. Most people who have third-house planets like physical movement and learning new things. Sitting still and being cooped up without room to move can affect third-house people in negative ways, even into adulthood.

You become restless when stuck in a basic routine; enjoyment comes from traveling, even if it's just a short distance. For example, you are content with short-distance travel like driving to a nearby town or commuting to a different area. Zoning out and feeling restless makes it difficult for you to relax and unwind. Having planets in the third house creates an abundance of energy that can also cause problems sleeping. Finding time to balance your professional and personal life helps reduce stress.

Socializing and meeting new people is exciting for you, and sharing common interests helps you build connections. If you have planets in the third house, you likely have an increased intelligence and a special ability to remember and recall information. Everywhere you go, you are spreading information and enlightening others with your intellect and wisdom, which brings other people happiness. However, it is important for you to learn to keep secrets and avoid participating in gossip.

Everything related to early childhood education, such as reading and basic education, is associated with the third house. Third-house people are born with natural writing abilities, which makes it easier for you to express yourself in a variety of ways. You are gifted with eloquent speaking, lecturing, and teaching abilities, and it is easy for you to make high-level information understandable to the average person. You are likely attracted to career fields such as journalism, publishing, radio, media, editing, and television, and you will succeed in any of these types of jobs because expressing your thoughts is how you create a sense of stability. You also might excel at working with your hands in creative endeavors such as carpentry, fixing cars, or doing household projects. As a third-house person, you like to study subjects that are interesting to you and rebel against being forced to learn about things that you find boring.

Planets in the Third House
If you have one or more planets in the third house, read the corresponding section for tips for transformation, healing, and resilience.

Sun in the Third House
You are a person who enjoys communicating and learning new things. You are gifted at connecting with people, and your charisma attracts others. Relationships with siblings play an important role in your life and friends become like family. Because your sun is in the third house, you shine when expressing your thoughts and pursuing intellectual interests. Expanding your knowledge, taking classes, reading the newspaper, and being educated about what is happening in the world brings you

happiness. Movement is also important for your happiness, and frequent travel helps balance your restless nature.

Moon in the Third House

You find personal security and comfort in educational and intellectual pursuits. Allow time to take short journeys and make travel a part of your daily routine, even if it's just taking the long way home. Freedom to roam and move around in your environment is important for your emotional well-being.

Realize that your emotions go through many phases and are always changing. Express intuitive feelings through writing and journaling. Although you may appear emotionally detached sometimes, you are able to balance your unstable emotions and intellectualize them. Emotional stability is tied to the ability to communicate with others. Because you were born with natural communication skills, you have a gift for sharing your feelings with others and being able to explain things well. Be cautious about overthinking feelings or stressing about things that are not important.

Mercury in the Third House

You need to know many things and crave continuous educational opportunities. Mercury is at home in the third house and enhances the gift of communication. You are eloquent and a natural salesperson. Blessed with a natural writing ability, you are able to analyze the smallest details and would also be a great editor. Intellectually stimulating conversations motivate you and help reduce boredom. Restlessness can be a problem if you are not able to travel and take short journeys. Finding the time to take classes and learn new things is important with this placement.

Venus in the Third House

You are charming and have pleasant relationships with your siblings. You have a love for literature, so reading and writing can increase your intellectual knowledge. When you were growing up, early childhood education was likely to be peaceful and fulfilling for you. Because you are imaginative and creative, pursuing artistic projects brings you happiness.

Venus in the third house creates a soft-spoken nature that attracts peaceful and intelligent partners. Developing and nurturing harmonious relationships with others comes naturally. Learning to express yourself in relationships will help you overcome feelings of shyness. Traveling short distances and socializing with neighbors is a big part of your daily routine.

Mars in the Third House

You are a person who speaks bluntly when expressing your opinions. You are assertive when communicating your feelings and are known to fight for your beliefs; nothing stops you from pursuing what you want. Be cautious about communicating with others when you're upset or angry. Avoid arguing by stepping away and calming down to avoid saying things you might later regret.

Sometimes you experience conflicts due to your strong opinions and beliefs and your directness. Some people might be afraid of communicating with you, especially if they disagree with your opinions. Winning arguments is not worth losing your friendships. Feeling connected to your family and neighbors is important to you. Addressing any anger felt toward your family members and mending those relationships will help encourage healing.

When Mars is in the third house, you passionately search for knowledge and have a desire to find answers to complex problems. Because you pursue adventure and need movement, traveling is especially beneficial for you.

Jupiter in the Third House

You feel knowledge is something noble and respect intellectual studies. Expanding your own intellect is something that comes naturally. Success and good luck in your educational pursuits helps you obtain future goals. It is important that you don't feel restricted and have the ability to move freely.

Allow yourself the freedom to move and travel as much as possible. Foreign travel is a big part of this placement because Jupiter in the third house signifies you are on a never-ending search for meaning and purpose in life. This placement encourages growth through experience.

Saturn in the Third House

You may feel insecure about expressing your ideas, thoughts, and opinions. Facing fears about being judged by others will help facilitate healing. It is important to heal past karmic issues regarding a lack of self-esteem. Learn to break down barriers that prevent open communication with others. Feeling responsible for your siblings, fulfilling the role of a parent, and taking on additional responsibilities is common with Saturn in the third house. Focus on the positive things in life and pay attention to your attitude. Shifting negative thoughts to positive ones can make a huge difference in your life.

Uranus in the Third House

You have a very eccentric personality and are curious about life. As an original thinker, you express your creativity through communication. It is important to make time to develop your innovative writing talents. Make time to pursue unique hobbies, talents, and interests. Express and pursue your natural teaching abilities. Dare to be different and make sure to share your amazing perspective with others, even if you don't think they will understand. Standing out from the crowd and adapting to unexpected changes in the environment is a strength of yours.

Neptune in the Third House

You are a person born with natural artistic abilities and someone who loves to daydream. With Neptune in the third house, you prefer to live in your imagination rather than considering practical ideas. It is important to live in the real world instead of trying to escape your responsibilities.

Mystical and dreamy, other people never quite understand what you are thinking. You might experience emotional pain due to miscommunication or illusions concerning other people. Try to work on overcoming secretiveness in relationships by communicating your true feelings instead of hiding them. Work on addressing unpleasant feelings and conflicts with siblings.

This is a powerful position for pursuing anything creative such as writing, theater, screenwriting, or poetry.

Pluto in the Third House

You are a perceptive person and can see through others' words easily. You're a powerful speaker who dislikes superficiality and prefers direct, honest communication. It is important to express your deepest emotions by writing and teaching others about things that matter. Healing comes through deep conversations and learning to be more vulnerable with others. This placement forces you to learn how to trust others and to share your thoughts and insights. Opening up about secrets, problems, and ideas and sharing them with family and friends is beneficial.

With Pluto in the third house, it is common for you to experience massive emotional deaths and rebirths involving your belief systems and opinions. Short journeys and travel can bring growth, change, and upheaval.

Cancer & the Fourth House

Nickname: Cancer the Mother

Symbol: The crab

Sun Sign Dates: June 22–July 22

Ruler: Moon

Rules: The fourth house; the breasts and stomach

Sign Type: Water, cardinal

Polar Opposite Sign: Capricorn

Tips for Healing: Express creativity, nurture the self, enjoy family time

C ancer is a cardinal sign, which means Cancerians are initiators who come up with new ideas and like to start projects.
As a water sign, they are born intuitive and have natural psychic
abilities. Cancer is a mothering sign, nurturing to all who cross
their path. At first glance they may seem private, serious, and
unemotional. This is because Cancerians hide their feelings; they
are deeply sensitive. They are actually very caring and concerned
about the welfare of others. Cancerians benefit when they learn
to learn to trust others and loosen their grip on them. Making
time to withdraw from social situations and spending time alone
are important for self-care. Having a shell protects their sensitive, caring, soft interior and camouflages fears of being hurt.

CHALLENGING ATTRIBUTES OF A CANCER

Because Cancer is ruled by the moon, they are affected greatly
by the lunar phases. It's important to acknowledge the powerful
effect the moon has on their emotions. During a full moon Cancerians may feel more irritable, moody, and depressed.

Just like the tides of the ocean, a Cancer's emotions go through
highs and lows. It is common for Cancerians to experience sadness, anxiety, and loneliness more than other water signs. Easily
hurt, they are extremely sensitive to how other people treat them.

As the emotional worrier of the zodiac, Cancerians often
focus on issues involving security. They crave emotional security
and worry about those they care about. They are also known to
control people and can be possessive of those they care about,
which is usually due to a self-esteem issue.

Resisting change is common for a Cancer because they work
hard to avoid feeling uncomfortable. They often find it difficult

to fully trust others no matter how long they have known them; this is an issue that Cancerians need to heal.

POSITIVE ATTRIBUTES OF A CANCER

Cancerians are creative and enjoy solitary activities like reading, writing, sewing, and journaling. When Cancerians are stressed out they have a strong need to retreat from the world, escaping to the safety of the home and their imagination. They are happiest when they are cozy inside the safety of their home and cuddling with their favorite pet.

One way a Cancer handles stress is by living in the past, daydreaming about how things used to be. They have an excellent memory, especially about things that happened in the past. Cancerians enjoy reminiscing and are nostalgic about places, people, and experiences. Be aware that collecting things can lead to hoarding tendencies because Cancerians are emotionally attached to possessions and find it hard to release them.

Cancerians enjoy working with children in some way, and there are two main reasons for this. First, they love the innocence of children and appreciate feeling needed. Second, children bring out their natural motherly instincts and allow them to express their nurturing personality. Children are innocent, kind, accepting, and affectionate, so Cancerians don't have to put up their hard shell around them. Cancer is drawn to the helping professions such as nursing, social work, and childcare because nurturing others is a natural gift.

Cancerians have a soothing presence and are easy to connect with because they understand other people's feelings. They are known as the caretakers of the zodiac. Taking care of those they love and doing things for them is their greatest talent. When they find someone that they can trust and open up to, they will do anything for them and are an extremely loyal friend. When someone close to them is sick, they naturally want to help take care of them and nurse them back to health. One of Cancer's strengths is being able to understand what other people need emotionally and then providing that support. Because this sign is ruled by the moon, it is associated with motherly energy, and most Cancerians typically have a strong connection with their own mother. Childhood experiences have a strong impact on Cancer, for better or for worse.

Cancerians are born with an ability to connect with others that are struggling. As a water sign, they are naturally empathic and can sense when someone is hurting. Sometimes this ability leads to feeling other people's pain. Because of this, Cancerians must find time to withdraw from the world and recover their energy after helping others. Having a secure home base and spending time alone helps a Cancer cope with social situations and familial obligations. Cancerians are the best nurturers and healers of the zodiac, but it is important for them to remember to make time to take care of their own needs.

Cancerians are known to have amazing intuition and can use their natural psychic abilities to find answers to many of life's problems. Trusting themselves and not ignoring that inner voice is key. Learning to listen to gut instincts before making decisions will help prepare Cancer for anything.

Relationships with a Cancer

Cancerians are homebodies. They like to retreat from society, so their home needs to be safe and comfortable. It is crucial for Cancerians to have a stable, loving home environment to return to or they may struggle to function in the real world. Spending time with family, cooking meals and taking care of their physical and emotional needs, makes Cancerians happy. But they also enjoy spending time alone; this is important for balancing emotions. Be mindful that if Cancerians refuse to spend time in social situations or to leave home, they begin to feel isolated. This can lead to increased feelings of depression and loneliness.

Cancerians are known to prefer one or two close friends in their lives. They can experience insecurity in relationships, especially when they are in love. There is a possessive and needy side to their personality. They become attached to others and prefer to spend their time with those they love. Cancerians experience jealousy when their loved ones spend time with other people. High expectations of others and expecting others to only want to be with them can lead to relationship difficulties. Learning to allow those they care about to have other relationships that don't include them is a learning lesson. Trusting others takes time for Cancerians.

Cancer Tips for Transformation

Cancerians transform when they are able to overcome insecurities and negative emotions. As a naturally shy person, they often have difficulties trusting others. Transforming into a more confident person happens when they find ways to manage their negative habits. Allowing caring people into their inner circle will help a Cancer become more trusting, compassionate, and understanding. They also need to remember that mothering people is not always necessary, and they need to nurture and take care of themselves too.

Focus on Positive Outcomes

Cancerians have a tendency to obsess and worry about all the things that could go wrong in life. Worries revolving around security—such as potential financial problems, losing their job, or suffering from health problems—are at the forefront of their mind. Being prepared helps Cancerians feel in control of things that might personally impact their life, but focusing on negative situations actually attracts negative experiences. When a Cancer realizes the impact their thoughts have on their emotions, they can start to deliberately change their behavior. Transformation occurs when they choose to focus on positive outcomes.

Trust in Others and in the Universe

Cancerians transform when they trust others enough to share their problems with them. If they try to protect themselves from being hurt, they will end up isolated, which prevents others from getting to know them. Realizing that controlling behavior actually makes life harder helps a Cancer grow and develop greater strength.

Trusting something larger than themselves and developing faith or a spiritual path creates peace. Cancerians need to remember that things happen for a reason and allow that peace to fill their heart; this will help relieve stress. Believe that good things will happen.

Leave Home

Cancerians are prone to giving up on their dreams because they avoid change and resist taking risks. Sometimes stepping into the unknown is when they grow the most. Venturing away from where they were raised will transform a Cancer into a more independent person. It is important for a Cancer not to live in the same house or town as their mother or family just because they feel guilt or a sense of duty. If a Cancer does choose to stay close to family, they need to make sure not to sacrifice their own happiness.

CANCER TIPS FOR HEALING

Healing begins when Cancerians nurture their own needs by focusing on their dreams, goals, hobbies, and interests. If they refuse to implement self-care in their life, burnout can happen. Learning to balance their giving nature by setting boundaries enables them to help others in a healthy way.

Trust Others

Cancerians do not like to feel vulnerable and are afraid of trusting others with their heart. Spending too much time focusing on old hurts can hold them back from finding true love. Learning to trust others helps lower their hard shell of protection. Healing comes when they take the risk of being in a relationship and experiencing intimacy. Sharing intimacy with someone can be one of the scariest things for Cancer, but it is also the fastest way for them to heal their wounds. Stepping out of their comfort zone and slowly allowing others into their private world is the first step to healing trust issues.

Balance Familial Responsibilities

Cancerians are known to spend a lot of time taking care of everyone else. They are often the one who visits family members in a nursing home—or moves them into their own home so they can be a caretaker. Taking on too many familial responsibilities and juggling these duties can be burdensome. Addressing the karmic learning within their family is important so they can heal.

Since Cancer is associated with the fourth house of home and family, they often feel responsible for their parents. They feel a sense of duty when it comes to family. At some time in their lives, they find themselves taking care of their parents either physically, emotionally, or financially. Even if there are older siblings nearby, a Cancer is typically the one who steps in to nurture and care for the needs of family. It is important for Cancerians to realize that while helping family is noble, it shouldn't become a burden; their own needs, their spouse, and their children should be the focus. Cancerians need to remember that if they don't take care of themselves first, it is difficult to truly assist others. Cancerians need to learn not to take on everyone else's problems.

Heal the Past

When Cancerians heal the past by letting go of the pain that they have experienced, they grow stronger as a person. Cancerians need to shift their focus to the present, let go of the past, and spend time planning for the future. Living in the past and replaying memories will cause stagnation. The past is over, and Cancerians must learn to move forward.

Worry Less

A Cancer's vulnerable areas are the chest, breasts, and stomach. When they are stressed, they can suffer from indigestion. Certain foods can aggravate the digestive system, such as dairy, causing flatulence. Due to emotional worrying, there are often stomach problems and bowel issues. Some Cancerians develop breast lumps and fibroid cysts, so it is important to visit the doctor regularly. Modifying their diet by cutting sugary sweets will make a big difference in how Cancerians feel.

CANCER RESILIENCY

It is important for a Cancer to adapt to challenges head on instead of avoiding discomfort. When adversity strikes, Cancerians naturally want to withdraw to the safety of the home, but they need to remember not to hide too long. Resiliency occurs when Cancerians face the world and live in it. They have the strength and patience to fight any battle, especially when they are doing things for family and ensuring their safety. Being needed by others helps motivate them to fight for what is important. Staying comfortable is fine, but Cancerians need to take small risks, adapt to change, and believe in themselves.

HOW TO SUPPORT A CANCER

When there is a Cancer in your life, always be there when they ask for help. Be supportive and reliable. Encourage them to be themselves and allow them to share how they feel. Help them self-reflect when they experience emotional highs and lows. Listen to them and ask them what they need. Be kind and give them time to figure things out. Don't pressure them because it causes anxiety and worry. Show them you can be trusted.

CANCER REFLECTION QUESTIONS

- What helps when you feel depressed or sad?
- How do you recover from feeling emotionally drained?
- Is there anything you need to heal?
- What personality traits help you become more resilient?
- How do you handle stress and anxiety?

CANCER AFFIRMATIONS

- "Everything happens at the perfect time for the good of all."
- "I like to spend time alone. I trust those I love."
- "I am accepted by the people I care about."
- "I balance my emotions. I think positive."

CANCER SELF-CARE IDEAS

- Prepare your favorite meal and spend time with family.
- Make time to express your creative side through journaling, listening to music, or creating art.
- Read a book that you have always wanted to read.
- Create three positive affirmations to recite daily.
- List three self-care techniques you find helpful and make time to do those things.
- Draw a flower with seven petals. Write down one new self-care activity you want to implement in each of the petals.

Then hang the flower on the wall as a reminder. Try to do one new self-care activity every day until you've incorporated them into your routine.

THE FOURTH HOUSE

Many of us remember the house we grew up in and the neighborhood friends we had when we were younger. We might reminisce about the times we played basketball with a sibling or the kid down the street whom we had a crush on. But the thing we usually remember the most is what type of childhood we had, especially when it comes to our parents and life inside our home. The fourth house symbolizes all the issues related to childhood, including our upbringing and our relationship with our parents. Depending on what planets are in the fourth house, you can tell a lot about your relationship with your mother and if there were issues involving nurturing.

I feel the fourth house is one of the most important houses psychologically because it is so important to our growth. As children we need a safe, secure, comfortable, reliable, and structured environment to thrive in. If home life or surroundings change or are unpredictable, it can have a devastating impact well into our adult years. The important lesson of the fourth house is for us to find our true home. We have the power and free will to change our future and make our current home as comfortable and happy as we can imagine.

Cancer rules the fourth house and represents mothering energy. There is a tendency toward isolation when planets are placed in this house. Fourth-house energy forces us to withdraw, hibernate, and isolate ourselves from the stresses of everyday life. It forces us to create a home base to work from and a place to rest when life gets tough. The goal of the fourth house is to push us into the future by encouraging us to find a safe haven where we can truly express ourselves.

If you don't have planets in the fourth house, this is not a bad thing. To find out more about the energy that impacts your childhood, parents, and family, you will need to look at the sign that sits on the cusp of your fourth house. For instance, if Sagittarius is on your fourth house cusp, you might have moved a lot as a child and possibly lived overseas. The home environment was a place where you had freedom to explore, study, and learn new things.

If You Have Planets in the Fourth House

The fourth house reveals a lot about your childhood home, current home, and future home. The different types of childhood experiences can be seen by looking at the sign on the fourth house cusp as well as planets placed here. Planets in the fourth house heighten the need to establish a safe and comfortable home life. Known to be caring, kind, sympathetic, and private, fourth-house people are strongly connected to parents and childhood friends.

Your personality is molded by family experiences in a deep way. You have a deep connection to people from your past. You also have a tendency to hold on to memories, feelings, and experiences. It can be hard to truly leave home and move away from immediate family. Depending on what planets are placed in this house, there is often karmic learning and healing that must be done regarding your relationships with family members.

When planets are in the fourth house, your mother has an important role in your life. Experiencing a strong bond with your mother figure is common. If your family life was unstable grow-ing up, perhaps due to your parents divorcing or separating, then emotional pain and suffering are common. You likely feel a strong sense of duty to take care of your mother, father, or grandparents. At some time in your life, you may be the one who has to take care of your parents' health issues or their everyday needs and finances. Even if you have siblings who live close by, you are often the one who steps into the caretaker role. Since most of your energy is focused on family, remember not to neglect yourself.

It's important for you to make time to nourish your soul by spending time at home doing solitary activities. Planets in the fourth house often indicate that you find enjoyment in cooking or baking for those you care about. Intuitive and imaginative at heart, you also benefit from expressing yourself through writing. Expressing emotions in some way is critical for you to obtain happiness. Believe in your artistic abilities; this helps build greater self-esteem, which is the key to coming out of your shell.

If you don't live alone, you would benefit by having a special room or space in your home that is just yours—one where you can relax and get away. Doing this helps you recover your energy after social interactions, which is paramount for balancing mind, body, and spirit.

Because you were born with natural parental instincts, you can find greater happiness by having children of your own. Cer-tain planets might restrict having children or make it difficult to conceive, such as Saturn in the fourth house. Whether you want to have children or not, working with children in a career such as teaching or childcare can bring contentment.

You want to please everyone in your family, which can make it difficult for you to prioritize your romantic life. Learning to balance your family and your current intimate relationships will take some effort. Showing affection to those closest to you can be difficult; you feel more comfortable showing love and affection to children and animals. Being able to trust others' intentions and getting out of your comfort zone will help heal relationships.

Fourth-house people are sentimental and remember everything that has happened in the past. Many people with planets in the fourth house continue to live with their parents during college and beyond. You need to focus on living in the present moment. If you learn to let go of painful, hurtful memories, this helps encourage forgiveness.

PLANETS IN THE FOURTH HOUSE

If you have one or more planets in the fourth house, read the corresponding sections for tips for transformation, healing, and resilience.

Sun in the Fourth House

You are a person who needs a happy, stable home life and enjoys spending time at home. A loving, happy, open home helps you thrive. Reminiscing about positive childhood memories is common with this placement. Repressing negative childhood memories and only focusing on positive experiences helps overcome past pain. If you experienced upheaval or conflict in your childhood home, it can affect your ability to trust. Establishing a stable, firm home base is critical for you to recharge and find happiness.

Motherly, nurturing, and sensitive, you enjoy taking care of those you care about. Because you are so connected to the past, you likely chose to live close to family or to move back to your hometown area. It is important to focus on your own home and family as an adult; make that your priority.

Having a father figure is paramount in your life, so it's wise to heal that relationship.

Moon in the Fourth House

You are a person who has strong feelings and emotions. Emotional happiness comes from your home environment. Interacting with family members and having a safe, secure, and reliable home base is critical for your emotional stability. Having a strong connection to your mother figure is important for your emotional development. You make your mother's needs a priority and sometimes neglect your own life. Because you are deeply connected to your parents, it can be difficult to leave home.

This placement intensifies the need to withdraw to recover from emotional stress. The moon in the fourth house influences fluctuations in mood, and experiencing highs and lows is common with this placement. Learning to express your deep emotional nature through writing or journaling can help you balance your emotions.

Mercury in the Fourth House

You are a person who spends a lot of time thinking about your home life. Communicating with family members and working through disagreements comes naturally. When Mercury is here, there is a need to communicate deeply with those you care about, and you regularly socialize with family members. Throwing parties and spending time with people you can intellectually debate with stimulates your mind. It is likely that one of your parents was seen as detached and intellectual instead of emotionally supportive. Journal about your feelings and control your tendency to overthink; this helps you avoid anxiety and worry.

Venus in the Fourth House

Fond of your roots, Venus in the fourth house means you value family traditions. As a child you were extremely close to one parent who was patient, gentle, and kind. Harmonious relationships are important with this placement; you have a tendency to avoid conflict with others.

You want your home to be pleasant and beautiful. This placement encourages a desire to decorate and make the home a beautiful place. Entertaining others and socializing at home brings happiness. Venus here inspires and is focused on giving love. With Venus in the fourth house, your children and spouse should come first.

Mars in the Fourth House

You like to dominate your home and be in charge. Often irritable and easily angered, you need to be careful about lashing out at loved ones. The home should be a peaceful place, not a place full of tension. If you don't control your strong drive and domineering nature, you can be seen as argumentative and combative. Fighting for the underdog in the family and aggressively defending those you care about is a strength. Find a way to balance your need to control your home environment and family members. Make time to actively communicate hurt feelings and heal your damaged family relationships.

There is often a family history of anger with this placement, and that can manifest by creating conflict with loved ones. Mars in the fourth house can sometimes indicate a childhood where some type of violence occurred in the home. Experiencing power struggles with your parents or witnessing power struggles between them is common.

Jupiter in the Fourth House

There is a chance your parents were financially wealthy and that you experienced a happy childhood. You are open-minded and generous with family, but sometimes you sacrifice your own needs to ensure others have what they need. This placement blesses you with a generous personality, so helping others becomes your role in the family. Taking in people who need protection brings you happiness.

You are a person who wants an open, large, and welcoming home. You exude optimism, which helps you attract great things. You will find that abundance overflows in life, bringing good luck and good fortune. Jupiter in the fourth house means you will enjoy a spacious home with an ability to move freely; living in a foreign country is common with this placement. You may own more than one home. You enjoy vacationing somewhere away from your main domicile.

Saturn in the Fourth House

You are a person who grew up in a traditional family. Childhood struggles impacted your view of financial security and emotional expression. One parent was strict, domineering, and limited the expression of love. You felt you had to grow up fast; duties and responsibilities were often the focus growing up. Work on accepting that you can have children and responsibilities without feeling burdened and unhappy. Because you were born with a karmic sense of duty to take care of family, it's crucial that you also relax within the home. Make time to have fun and do things with family and friends that bring joy. Karmic wounds that are passed down from generation to generation need to be healed.

Uranus in the Fourth House

You are a person who experiences sudden changes in your home life. Growing up, you felt detached and different from your family. There might have been constant moving or changes of residence. With Uranus in the fourth house, experiencing one parent as detached, unstable, or distant is common. This position often indicates parental divorce or loss of a family member in early life.

This placement shows a rebellion against traditional family values and someone who seeks their own path. Unexpected upheaval in childhood led you to believe that you can't have security as an adult. The home should be secure and stable, but if that was not experienced, you may find it hard to settle down. Express your creative, eccentric nature by decorating your home with unique items. Make efforts to create a stable and balanced home life. Healing your desire for chaos and drama within the home will bring greater stability.

Neptune in the Fourth House

You are a person who is highly sensitive to the emotional undercurrents in the home. One of your parents may have struggled with addiction to alcohol or drugs, and this affected you emotionally. It is also common for people with this placement to take on the role of caretaker and help a parent who struggles with physical illness or mental health issues. Family secrets were a common part of your childhood and often affect your adult life. Your childhood was likely filled with illusions and suffering due to your sensitive nature. Overcome illusions that clouded the truth about your childhood home by taking off rose-colored glasses when it comes to your loved ones; learn to forgive.

This placement increases psychic abilities and artistic talents. Neptune in the fourth house also creates a strong desire to withdraw from the practical world. You have a reclusive nature and like spending time at home by yourself. You can heal your childhood experiences by finding an artistic outlet, expressing mystical feelings, and having a compassionate home base. Living by the ocean or near water can bring comfort and healing.

Pluto in the Fourth House

Your childhood was permeated by feelings of deep change, with constant loss and endings. With Pluto in the fourth house, it is common to experience the death of a close family member during childhood. This placement indicates that you felt unsafe or unsettled during childhood. There might have been a feeling that something bad was going to happen or you were always waiting for something unexpected to happen. There was often intense tensions within the home where you were unable to stand up for yourself due to a controlling parent. You often had power struggles with your parents and pushed the limits during your teenage years, which brought conflict. There are family secrets that might have been exposed when you were older because of your desire to dig deeper to know the truth. Constant upheaval in the home environment is not healthy, and you need to learn to create a balanced home life.

You are a person who has a deep need to transform and grow. Heal your childhood pain by forgiving others and moving on from the past. Nurture and heal wounds surrounding neglect, betrayal, the death or loss of a close family member, or abuse at the hands of someone you trusted. Allow your adult home to regenerate your energy, creating greater resilience.

CHAPTER

Leo & the Fifth House

Nickname: Leo the Performer

Symbol: The lion

Sun Sign Dates: July 23–August 22

Ruler: Sun

Rules: The fifth house; the heart and spine

Sign Type: Fire, fixed

Polar Opposite Sign: Aquarius

Tips for Healing: Praise yourself, allow others to shine, have fun

Leo is a fixed sign, which means Leos are strong-willed, stubborn, determined, and resistant to change. Being ruled by the element of fire makes them naturally energetic, dramatic, flirtatious, warm, social, childlike, and creative. Once others get to know a Leo, they realize that behind the roar of the lion exists an innocent child wanting attention. Leos are known for their passion, charm, and charisma; they are the most charming sign in the zodiac. They have a generous spirit and a big heart. Leos make excellent friends and are very protective of their family.

CHALLENGING ATTRIBUTES OF A LEO

If Leos feel ignored, they will force their energy on others because they want to make sure they are noticed. Ruled by the sun, being the center of the Universe is when Leos feel their best. The natural energy of this sign is powerful and draws the attention of many people.

Because Leos are extremely hardworking, seeing the big picture is easy for them, but they struggle with disorganization, which can be challenging. Working with others who are more organized and asking others to help prioritize tasks will help Leos achieve many goals.

A Leo's impulsive behavior can aggravate the people in their life; it's hard for Leo to follow anyone else's rules or expectations. Being ruled by the sun enhances their need to be in the limelight and to be in charge. When a Leo makes up their mind to do something, no one can convince them otherwise. As a fixed sign, they can be strong-willed and self-absorbed at times, acting on their own volition and not discussing their plans with others. Those closest to them can try to give them practical advice, but many Leos find it hard to incorporate other people's ideas. It can be difficult for Leos to take advice from others because they believe it is a sign of weakness. Leos like to be in positions of authority. Being a leader is something they are meant to master, but this requires them to allow others to be in the limelight too.

Positive Attributes of a Leo

Leo energy rules the fifth house, which is associated with love affairs, gambling, creativity, and children. Naturally artistic and extremely creative, Leos have many talents. Lots of famous musicians, actors, politicians, and writers have this sun sign. Leos love to perform in front of a crowd. This can take many forms for Leos; they may pursue teaching, public speaking, acting, or politics.

At first glance Leos appear confident, refined, and dignified. They enjoy being in charge and giving orders. Being recognized and being in the limelight is important for them. Like a king or queen, they naturally obtain a position of power and lead others. They strive to obtain a position of authority because this makes them feel important and enhances their self-esteem. Born optimistic and happy, they do not stay depressed for very long. When faced with adversity, they rise up with strength and courage. Leos are born with courage, stamina, and the ability to work hard.

Leos overcome stressful times by focusing on the positive things in life and tapping in to their childlike innocence. They are known to love children and have a strong desire to become a parent. Leos may enjoy working with children in some way, even if they don't have children of their own. Children are naturally attracted to Leos because of their lively, playful, and fun nature.

Known for making people laugh, Leos are often the life of the party. They make excellent allies because they want people to like them and they care if others are truly happy. Feeling happy is crucial for a Leo to be successful. They are at their best when they feel loved, appreciated, recognized, admired, and respected. The best way to win a Leo's heart is to give them compliments.

RELATIONSHIPS WITH A LEO

In relationships Leos crave affection and are very romantic. With a flirtatious, fun nature, they have an ability to entice others into passionate love affairs. Getting what they want comes easily and other people like how Leos make them feel. It is hard for people not to like them because of their friendliness, good nature, and ability to make others feel special.

Struggles can surface in intimate relationships due to problems with commitment. On one hand they desire attention, love, and companionship, but on the other hand, they crave independence. It is sometimes hard to balance these competing needs. The moment Leos feel restrained or pinned down, they desire to break free. Leos need relationship partners that will cater to their needs but also allow them a lot of space. Many people believe that Leos are selfish and only think about their own needs. The truth is that Leos are one the most generous signs in the zodiac, but they need the freedom to pursue their own hobbies and interests. The perfect relationship partner for Leo is someone that gives them room to roam and encourages their creativity. It is important for a Leo's partner to understand their flirtatious nature and realize that they need a sense of excitement, challenge, and passion in relationships to feel alive.

Having relationships with others is how Leos find their greatest lessons and challenges. Leos tend to get wrapped up in their own accomplishments and can forget loved ones also need to feel important. If loved ones point this behavior out, Leos will make changes because they don't want to be viewed as self-centered or selfish. Leos care about how others perceive them and will work hard to change their behavior to make their loved ones happy.

LEO TIPS FOR TRANSFORMATION

Leos need to be noticed and appreciated for their talents. When they receive praise, it helps boost their self-esteem and inspires them to achieve more. Transformation occurs when Leos shift the focus to others and build them up with words, compliments, and recognition.

Praise Yourself

Learning to give themselves the praise they desire helps a Leo transform. They must allow inner validation; if Leos stop seeking approval from others and the outside world, they will find greater happiness. Believing in their talents and recognizing that they are special will help increase self-esteem. Leos need to focus on loving themselves and making themselves happy instead of worrying about the approval of others.

Compliment Others

Instead of waiting for compliments from others, Leo can start complimenting them; giving others the energy that they want themselves will bring that energy back to them. Leos need to learn to be more modest and to allow others to get the credit sometimes. When they master these abilities, they will transform many personal relationships.

Express Creativity

If Leos can learn how to express their creative gifts and utilize them, they will transform many areas of their life. Expressing creativity can involve sharing ideas with others, drawing, writing, acting, or participating in sports. Whatever artistic talents a Leo possesses, it's important to share them with the world. The more they express themselves, the more self-aware they will become. Transformation comes when Leo finds happiness within and stops seeking it in the outside world.

LEO TIPS FOR HEALING

Healing a deep-seated need to always be the best at everything makes Leos healthier and happier. They will feel lighter and like a weight is lifted off their shoulders when they stop caring so much about what others think.

Share Recognition

Leos work hard and are talented in many areas, but always seeking approval can be draining and exhausting. Sharing positive feedback with someone else can be one of the fastest ways to heal their wounds.

Receiving recognition is linked to a Leo's identity and influences their self-esteem. Leos do not like to feel ignored and need constant attention to feel good about themselves. Sharing recognition can be challenging, but Leos need to learn to allow others to have a turn in the limelight. They need to avoid being in competition with others, especially their coworkers.

Find Love

Finding true love and romance is something that can heal a Leo's heart. They struggle with commitment in relationships and need to change self-focused behaviors. The first step is learning to balance their desire for freedom with their desire to be taken care of and loved. Healing begins when Leo realizes they can have both.

Staying present and healing past relationship wounds helps Leos realize the benefits of being committed to one person. Leos need to remember there are things that can be done to spice up relationships; they don't need to move on to the next person as soon as things get boring. Learning that friendship is what builds a solid foundation in romantic relationships will help them along the way.

Spend Time with Children

Leos are children at heart and have a naive emotional nature. Being around children can be comforting and healing. Becoming a parent and spending time with children helps a Leo learn about themselves, increases self-esteem, heals inner child issues, and utilizes their creativity. If a Leo is unable to have children of their own (or decides not to), then they would benefit from volunteering or working with children in some way.

Manage Stress

Stress can manifest in the body and lead to circulation problems and heart issues. Leos should take care of their heart by balancing their diet to control blood pressure and cholesterol. A Leo's vulnerable area is the back, and they can experience muscle tension and spasms. Upper back issues are common. Seeing a chiropractor or implementing stretching exercises might be helpful to prevent back pain.

LEO RESILIENCY

Leos have a childlike spirit. They possess an innocence and faith that is endearing. Leos have a strong personality, and it's important that they let their light shine. The passion and zeal they have for life is contagious. Larger-than-life personality traits impact others around them. Usually upbeat and friendly on the outside, underneath that persona Leos can feel stressed and anxious just like anyone else. The positive thing about Leos is that they do not stay depressed for very long. They push forward by doing something fun and exciting. Resiliency comes easily because they use social situations, spending time in public, and hanging out with friends to bounce back. Leos avoid isolating themselves because they dislike being alone, and this helps overcome negative feelings.

Helping other people encourages a Leo to become more resilient. Positive energy can be contagious, and Leos can help others who are struggling with depression, sadness, or anxiety. Leos bring out their playful side to uplift other people and make them laugh. They have a natural ability to make others feel special and deeply impact other people's lives.

Leos can find resilience by not taking things too personally and realizing they can't always be the most important person in the room. Giving up a need for other people's approval will help them become more resilient. It is important that Leos do not let their innocent heart be hurt by a perceived lack of attention or disapproval from others. They need to stop creating drama and chaos when not receiving the right amount of attention from loved ones; other people need love and affection too. If a Leo can give more to others instead of expecting others to give to them first, then they will find true happiness.

How to Support a Leo

When there is a Leo is in your life, treat them like they are the most important person in the world. Give them your undivided attention. Be a loyal and honest person. Praise them for their efforts and let them know you believe in them. Always give them encouraging and positive feedback. They get their feelings hurt easily, so be kind. Have fun by doing exciting things together. Allow them time to explore and give them the freedom to do things on their own.

Leo Reflection Questions

- What creative and artistic talents do you have?

- How do you make time to do things that make you happy?

- Is there anything you need to heal?

- What personality traits help you become more resilient?

- How do you handle stress and anxiety?

Leo Affirmations

- "I am creative. My creativity is one of my greatest strengths."

- "I am fun to be around and I enjoy helping others. I am a natural leader."

- "I heal myself and others with my sense of humor and positive attitude."

- "I am strong and resilient. I always look at the bright side of things."

LEO SELF-CARE IDEAS

- Spend time entertaining, socializing, and having fun with friends and family.

- Express your creative side. Take music lessons or art classes.

- Spend time with children.

- Create three positive affirmations to recite daily.

- List three self-care techniques you find helpful and make time to do those things.

- Draw a flower with seven petals. Write down one new self-care activity you want to implement in each of the petals. Then hang the flower on the wall as a reminder. Try to do one new self-care activity every day until you've incorporated them into your routine.

THE FIFTH HOUSE

The fifth house is an area of fun, pleasure, love affairs, excitement, sports, gambling, and recreation. It is associated with children and any issues related to being childlike. Experiencing the joy of becoming a parent and being responsible for raising a child is a fifth-house journey. This house is one of the happiest houses and brings a lightness of energy into our everyday lives. It is hard to find anything troubling about the fifth house because it is all about experiencing pleasure and enjoying life. Planets placed here will reveal an interest in being a parent or encourage a desire to work with children in some way.

The energy of this house reveals the creative side of life as well as the drive for self-expression. Leo the entertainer rules this house, and it is no surprise that planets placed here create an interest in music, writing, acting, or sports. Planets in the fifth house can show where we shine in the world and what type of talents we possess.

If you don't have planets in the fifth house, that is not a bad thing. You will need to look at the sign on the cusp of the fifth house to see what energy affects your creativity and self-expression. For instance, if Pisces is on the fifth house cusp, you have a vivid imagination and artistic abilities. You have an emotional need to express yourself through music, art, acting, and writing. Love affairs can be emotionally painful if you do not learn to develop stronger boundaries. Romantic, passionate, and idealistic in love, you will enjoy the newness of relationships.

If You Have Planets in the Fifth House

You are talented, flirtatious, domineering, and attention-seeking. You have a strong desire to express yourself in a bold way. You are naturally talented and blessed with special gifts; you know this and enjoy being recognized for your artistic abilities. Planets in the fifth house mean you crave attention and recognition, and you have a desire to be in the limelight.

Positive, fun-loving, and happy, you have a great zeal for life and want to enjoy every moment. Planets in the fifth house bring a need for excitement and adrenaline. You love the thrill of the chase. You like being surrounded by happy people and dislike being alone. Fifth-house people might have several short-lived romances and a string of heartbroken lovers. Your exes may say that you are self-absorbed and narcissistic. This isn't true, but you tend to withdraw and push others away if you feel you are not getting the attention you deserve. When you are not getting attention, praise, or recognition, you can become irritable, sad, and depressed. With planets in the fifth house, there is a focus on the self and a difficulty being aware of the needs of others. Taking deliberate action to change your behavior and develop greater self-awareness helps overcome self-centeredness. It is important for you to see yourself through another person's eyes. This helps balance a strong need for self-expression and redirects your energy to maintain healthy relationships.

You have a natural ability to attract others due to your sensual, romantic, and passionate nature. You desire passion, excitement, and love, so sometimes you find yourself entangled in a multitude of stormy love affairs with multiple lovers and a new date every weekend. You are flirtatious, attractive, playful, and enjoy being in love because it's new and inspiring. It is important that you know and understand yourself and your own needs or other people might get hurt by this behavior. People with fifth-house planets may unintentionally neglect the needs of loved ones.

If you are in a relationship with someone, others might misjudge your behavior, feeling that you are lacking a genuine commitment. In reality, you are just being yourself and expressing a fun-loving nature. Part of your personality is driven to explore and experience as many things as possible. When you are in a committed relationship with someone, it is extremely important for you to have romantic feelings, sexual attraction, and physical chemistry. You need to feel and express love strongly and boldly without restriction. The fifth-house journey is one of happiness, newness, and excitement.

This is the house of children. As long as your other placements are beneficial, becoming a parent and having several children will benefit you. Children are symbolic of creative talents and are something that can molded and perfected. Because you are so fond of children, you might pursue a career in teaching or work where you can help children in some way. Children are innocent, trusting, and naive—all traits that fifth-house people resonate with. Noticing someone else's talent and sharing it with the world brings you fulfillment.

Planets in the Fifth House

If you have planets in the fifth house, read the corresponding sections for tips for transformation, healing, and resilience.

Sun in the Fifth House

You are a positive person who needs self-expression and freedom to pursue anything that brings you pleasure. This is a great place for the sun; it is at home here and brings positive energy. Feeling alive and experiencing romance, fun, and excitement are important to you. Make sure to balance pursuits such as love affairs, partying, gambling, and other behaviors that can cause difficulties.

Make time to express your artistic talents. Creative, talented, and imaginative, you shine when on stage or in front of a crowd. Having children brings good luck, and being a parent helps you transform into a stronger person. Blessings come by surrounding yourself with energetic, positive people and learning to guard your energy.

Moon in the Fifth House

You have an intense emotional nature and need to feel love in personal relationships. The moon in the fifth house causes emotional fluctuations and imbalances. It may seem like you are very creative one minute and then at other times, you can't express yourself.

Experiencing passion and love make you feel alive. Raising children and spending time being playful brings you happiness. This placement creates an honest and genuine person who craves attention and recognition. Learn to express your true feelings with those you care about. Pursuing a talent such as music, singing, drawing, or participating in sports helps alleviate depression.

Mercury in the Fifth House

You have a strong drive to express your thoughts, opinions, and interests. Naturally gifted at writing, speaking, and teaching, you should create an outlet to express your thoughts in daily life. Mercury placed here needs to learn and communicate with others. You need romantic partners who can intellectually stimulate the mind; you need someone on your mental level. Working with children in some way and educating them about the world brings you happiness. Discussing many topics and interests with those you care about should be a priority. Because you are social, engaging, and entertaining, it is no surprise that other people love being in your presence. Recognize your need to be admired for your intelligence and creative talents. It is important to make time for writing and journaling your ideas.

Venus in the Fifth House

You are a person who is attractive and has a calming presence. Seeking pleasure, love affairs, romance, and fun helps bring satisfaction. Sometimes you feel torn when trying to please others and neglect your own needs. Make time in your life to enjoy good food, vacations, and parties, and surround yourself with nice things that bring you comfort.

Pursuing romance and passionate love affairs brings you comfort. Lavishing others with affection comes naturally, but you expect the same in return. You have a tendency to spoil your children and give them everything they want. It will be beneficial to balance your strong romantic desires and passions. Be cautious about overindulging in hobbies such as gambling, drinking, partying, and sexual relationships.

Mars in the Fifth House

If you don't balance your need for dominance, it can lead to conflicts and arguments that affect your relationships. You are forceful in expressing your needs, wants, and desires, and you have a powerful energy that makes others feel overwhelmed at times. However, Mars placed here is tempered with optimism, which helps settle your aggressive tendencies.

Be mindful that experiencing the feeling of being in love or experiencing a challenge should not be all that you are focused on. Sometimes overly demanding in relationships, you are known to push people away once conflict arises or when you don't get what you want. Relationships with others will improve once you learn not to take criticism or advice as a personal attack. Having children might cause feelings of unhappiness if you feel forced into heavy responsibilities that limit your ability to have fun. Experiencing tension and arguments with your children is common with this placement. Life improves once you learn to be more patient with yourself and others. Taming your enormous sexual appetite, desires, and romantic feelings can keep you from getting entangled in unhealthy, toxic relationships.

You are a person who expresses a strong, passionate nature. This placement creates athletic abilities and creative talents that can be used to excel in many endeavors. Utilize your powerful energy to achieve your creative goals and finish projects.

Jupiter in the Fifth House

You are a person who has good luck and is optimistic about life. You might have good luck when gambling and taking risks. Easygoing by nature, there is not a lot that rattles or upsets you. You're always willing to have fun, and pursuing things that bring joy such as travel and adventure will bring you happiness. You dislike restrictions; you are a free spirit who is always on an adventure to find new ways to express yourself.

Finding time to have fun and experiencing love affairs can sometimes be taken too far and become excessive. It is not uncommon to have many lovers from different cultural or social backgrounds. Jupiter here is prone to excess, so you need to balance your desires and appetites. It is important to allow frequent movement in your life and to share your enormous amount of energy and passion with others. This placement often indicates a large family with many children. Born with a big heart and generous nature, it is important to express your artistic talents.

Saturn in the Fifth House

This placement means life improves with time and age. You are a serious person who fears being judged and criticized. Feeling frustrated and unable to express yourself is common. There is a feeling of restriction in fifth-house areas of life such as love, romance, communication, and self-expression.

Because you are super responsible, you often end up taking care of other people's children. You might be drawn to teaching, childcare, or raising a family. Sometimes it is difficult to conceive or have children with this placement. As a parent, you have a tendency to be strict and expect your children to be overly responsible. Because you are easily embarrassed and private, you shy away from pursuing the traditional fun activities that rule the fifth house. If you can learn to trust your own artistic talents and stop being so hard on yourself, life will improve. Focus on healing any insecurities involving self-esteem, love, and vulnerability.

Uranus in the Fifth House

This placement creates a desire for self-expression that is shocking, eccentric, and unique. It is important for you to stand out in a crowd. You want to be known for your unique fashion style and creative ideas. Learning to nurture your creative and innovative talents will help you communicate your out-of-the-box ideas.

Uranus here creates a detached and freedom-loving person who dislikes feeling tied down by commitments. Leaving a string of hurt lovers behind you is common because of a tendency to unexpectedly end relationships for no reason. Intense and dramatic love affairs are common with Uranus here; so is a need to control chaotic partnerships. Unplanned pregnancies are common; if you have children, they will be highly intelligent and unique in some way.

You have a need for an unconventional and nontraditional love life; you may be better suited for an open relationship. Truthfulness and honesty are important in your romantic relationships, and you need to develop emotional stability. Learning patience and how to have relationships without feeling restricted is a lesson of this placement.

Neptune in the Fifth House

You are a person who appreciates art, spirituality, and romance. Neptune here has a gentle, romantic nature and loves beautiful music, poetry, and affection in general. Be careful about self-deception; make an effort not to see others through rose-colored glasses. You may attract emotionally unstable lovers who are unreliable and never there when you need them. Heartbreak is common when Neptune is in the fifth house because you have a strong urge to help others, even if they don't deserve it. This placement often leads to a restless search for true love, so make sure that your relationships are balanced and that you receive as much as you give.

Having your own children can bring happiness, and you will want to teach them how to express themselves through art and creativity. It is important to express your own artistic talents and spiritual nature.

Pluto in the Fifth House

You are a person who takes artistic pursuits seriously and possesses an intense amount of creative energy. With this placement, everything you pursue involving pleasure is serious and deliberate. You strive to attain all your goals in a determined, focused way and express your desires.

In love affairs, you are often intense, controlling, and possessive, and your feelings are all or nothing. This placement indicates you cut others off easily when you feel betrayed or are not interested anymore. Transformation comes when you fall in love, experience sexuality and intimacy, and pursue pleasure. It can be difficult for you to relax or have fun due to your serious nature, so being around more exciting lovers helps break down your inhibitions.

When you love someone, you can become obsessive and jealous. It is important to heal your intense need for powerful and unhealthy relationships. Being a parent is taken seriously, and once you have children, you will want to control them in some way. Express your intense passion through healthy hobbies and interests instead.

CHAPTER

Virgo & the Sixth House

Nickname: Virgo the Servant

Symbol: The maiden

Sun Sign Dates: August 23–September 22

Ruler: Mercury

Rules: The sixth house; the digestive system

Sign Type: Earth, mutable

Polar Opposite Sign: Pisces

Tips for Healing: Practice self-care, control over-thinking, balance your need for perfection

Virgo is a mutable sign, which means Virgos are adaptable, flexible, and able to accept change easily. They are the hardest workers of the zodiac and are known for their tedious work ethic, practicality, stability, and organizational abilities. At first glance Virgos might appear timid, shy, and quiet; some people think they are boring, prudish, and dull because of their reserved nature. Once people really get to know a Virgo, they realize they are friendly, talkative, and love to help others. Many astrology books make Virgos sound difficult, compulsive, irrational, and obsessed with details. But Virgo has the heart of a servant, and helping others is their gift. Virgos enjoy making things better, and part of their process is to try to make things perfect.

Mercury rules Virgo, making Virgos intelligent, analytical, and articulate. Everything that has to do with communication, intelligence, and knowledge is associated with the sign Virgo.

CHALLENGING ATTRIBUTES OF A VIRGO

Virgos are known to discuss the same experience or problem with friends over and over again, and they can obsess about something so much that others feel overwhelmed. A Virgo's active mind causes anxiety, and when they overthink and try to figure out why something happened or when they try to control the outcome of things, they experience stress. Sometimes Virgos find it difficult to broaden their perspective, which prevents them from seeing the bigger picture. It's important for Virgos to remember that not everything can be figured out; they can't always know why something occurred or happened the way that it did. Analyzing their own thoughts and emotions too much can affect a Virgo's mood and prevent happiness. It is important to learn how to take someone else's advice; being right is not the most important thing. Others might perceive them as picky and high-strung, so working on balancing these personality traits will help relationships improve.

As the perfectionist of the zodiac, Virgos are often hardest on themselves. Born with high standards that are almost impossible to live up to, they are very critical about mistakes, flaws, and nuisances in the environment. Criticism from others hurts a Virgo deeply because they have already analyzed their own faults and struggle to see things in a positive light. Virgos need to give themselves some grace. They don't take compliments well and need to learn self-love.

Virgos are known to be obsessive-compulsive. They are detail-focused and tend to overanalyze situations. They are also hypochondriacs when it comes to their health. They worry more than any other zodiac sign, which causes them to obsess about physical symptoms. They constantly fear getting sick.

We know Virgos like things to be a certain way (structured and organized!) and do best in a stable environment. Having a routine brings Virgo comfort, whereas change disturbs their overall peace of mind. A messy environment also causes a Virgo distress. Virgos find it hard to fully relax because they are often focused on small things in the environment that need to be fixed. For instance, if a picture is slightly crooked or if there are dishes in the sink, they'll straighten the picture and wash the dishes before they sit down on the couch to binge Netflix.

POSITIVE ATTRIBUTES OF A VIRGO

Virgos are known to have an amazing ability to communicate and explain complex subjects to others in a way they can understand. Being ruled by the planet Mercury increases intelligence and the ability to express themselves through oral and written communication. Meticulous and detail-oriented, Virgos are excellent writers or editors. The ability to zone in on the one misspelled word that everyone else missed can be a blessing and a curse.

Virgos are at their best when they are working and are known to finish their work in a timely manner. They are excellent teammates and excel when they are part of a dynamic team. They're happy to lend a hand to their coworkers or supervisors. With their heart always in the right place, they want to make sure things run smoothly and effortlessly.

Virgos need a peaceful environment when working, so working from home is a Virgo's dream. Having control over their surroundings helps Virgos feel grounded. It's also crucial for Virgos to have structure. Feeling safe and protected is important for their mental health. Avoiding drama and emotional upheaval and spending time alone is an important part of Virgo self-care. Virgos value privacy, so having a quiet place to read, journal, and write is key for their overall health.

Virgo rules the sixth house and issues related to structure, service, health, routine, and diet. They are destined to help others and take care of people in some capacity. Naturally caring as a person, Virgos enjoy taking care of those who are in need. Making a difference in people's lives leads them to careers such as nursing, medicine, accounting, social work, psychology, or another job that allows them to accomplish acts of service.

Task-oriented Virgos have an amazing ability to multitask; their high energy enables them to accomplish many things at once. Their coworkers and those closest to them often find it difficult to compete because of their ability to finish things quickly. Coworkers enjoy their company because they provide a listening ear and offer comfort by giving practical advice. Feeling needed gives Virgos a sense of purpose. Helping others comes naturally for a Virgo, and doing practical things for those they care about is how they show love. Modest and selfless at heart, Virgos do not serve others for admiration or acknowledgment. They prefer working behind the scenes, hidden away where there isn't much noise or disturbance.

RELATIONSHIPS WITH A VIRGO

Virgos are known as the feminine archetype of purity and innocence. They are extremely private, especially with matters of the heart. A Virgo could love someone and no one would ever know it. Virgos often struggle with intimacy issues; trusting others enough to have a physical or sexual relationship is a common learning lesson. They find it difficult to express their true feelings due to being introverted. On the other hand, they are good at expressing what they think about practical matters.

Virgos are often misjudged as cold, but once they begin to feel comfortable, that illusive detachment melts away. When a Virgo trusts someone, there is nothing they would not do for that person. Virgos are very giving and enjoy buying gifts and helping loved ones. They are loyal, trustworthy friends who can be counted on to be there when people they care about need them. They are reliable and responsible.

Many people live by the motto "If it ain't broke, don't fix it." That mentality causes Virgo stress and mental anguish; they believe that things can always be made more efficient. But Virgos can experience difficulties in relationships if others do not understand the changes they want to make.

Personality traits can manifest in different ways, but Virgos are known to obsess over emotions, and this can make relationships challenging. Sometimes they spend all of their time thinking about work and attaining a successful career, neglecting their personal relationships. They will benefit from controlling their negative thoughts and implementing mindfulness exercises to live in present moment.

Virgo Tips for Transformation

Trusting that things will work out the way they are meant to is crucial for a Virgo to find happiness. Virgos grow as a person by making an effort not to overwork themselves. They should take regular vacations and spend lots of quality time with loved ones.

Overcome Worry

Virgos need to realize that worrying about things will not change the outcome. They must learn to let go of negative thinking and their need for control. Once they overcome worry, Virgos will find peace and begin to trust in the process of life. Transformation happens when Virgos stop overanalyzing situations, emotions, and behaviors.

Balance Workaholic Tendencies

Virgos are known to be workaholics. Accomplishing tasks and achieving great things brings them contentment, but it could be at the expense of their own health. They transform when they start putting themselves first. It is healthy for Virgos to get off the computer and walk away from their work desk. Virgos should do some stretching and take a walk during their daily lunch break. Transformation occurs when Virgos realize that self-worth and happiness will never come from completing mundane tasks. It is important for Virgos to make time to relax away from work and to prioritize leisure activities. They find comfort in reading, writing, gardening, and spending time in nature.

Overcome Shyness

When Virgos learn to overcome shyness by stepping out of their comfort zone in social situations, they will transform. Sharing ideas with others and coming out of their shell will help them develop friendships. If Virgos stop worrying about what others think about them, they can become more self-confident. Being more open and allowing themselves to be vulnerable will also help them find someone to love. Virgos will change for the better when they realize there is much more to life than just working hard and achieving goals.

VIRGO TIPS FOR HEALING

Healing comes when Virgos learn how to say no. They have a natural desire to avoid conflict, which makes them commit to things when they shouldn't. It is common for them to give more than they receive. When they give too much of themselves, they will feel physically and emotionally drained.

Implement Self-Care

Virgos need to implement self-care more than any other zodiac sign. Pushing themselves to the limit and succumbing to burnout is common for Virgos. Stepping away from work and making time for vacation, travel, and adventure is important. Virgos reenergize by withdrawing, taking care of their own needs, and spending time alone, secluded from the hustle and bustle of the world. They need to implement self-care activities into their daily routine. As an earth sign, they will find that relaxation comes from cleaning, organizing their home, walking their dog, or spending time outdoors. They benefit from solitary activities such as reading, writing, creating, and cooking. Virgos can also recharge by spending time with close friends.

Control Your Thoughts

Virgos can heal when they learn to control their rambling thoughts. Their mind is always active and this can cause difficulty sleeping at night. If they wake up in the middle of the night, sometimes they start thinking about work or something they forgot to do, making it difficult to fall back to sleep. Implementing stress-management techniques in their daily routine will help Virgos achieve greater emotional balance. Virgos will feel healthier and sleep better if they learn to incorporate mindfulness techniques into their day-to-day life. Practicing deep breathing exercises, yoga, and meditation is also beneficial. Many Virgos find that writing their ideas down in a journal is helpful because it is a way to get unwanted thoughts out of their head.

Stay Grounded in the Present

Virgos are known to obsess compulsively about things out of their control. Thinking too much about the future and worrying can trap a Virgo in an endless cycle of depressive thoughts. Learning to stay grounded in the moment allows them to be fully present when they are completing activities. They can do this by focusing on their breathing and doing activities like Tai Chi, stretching, and other movement exercises to connect to their physical body. Walking in nature barefoot and feeling the dirt beneath their feet can help ground them. Gardening and spending time outside growing herbs and plants will help reduce stress. They benefit through practicing mindfulness exercises and practical outlets like journaling, taking a walk, or cuddling with their favorite pet. Virgos can find peace, relaxation, and greater work-life balance when they learn to stay grounded in the present moment.

Relax

Virgos' vulnerable area is the stomach. Excessive worry can cause acid reflux issues and nausea. Stomach ulcers and indigestion happen when Virgos are stressed out about things, so it's important to learn how to ease anxiety with antacids, essential oils, or whatever will help relax and calm the nerves. If Virgos suffer from anxiety, worry, restlessness, this could lead to insomnia. Finding time to unwind before bed is important; Virgos should avoid activities that stimulate the mind, such as scrolling on their phone or watching television.

Virgo Resiliency

When difficult things happen, Virgos are like rescue workers that swoop in and give everything they have to help others. Adapting to crisis situations is something they do well. Never asking for anything in return, they need to make sure to find a healthy balance in giving. Resiliency comes easily when a Virgo releases their need for perfection and worries about the future. They need to appreciate what they have and be grateful for the positive things in their life. If Virgos are obsessing about negative things, they can adapt and move forward by focusing on helping those in need. Feeling needed and appreciated by others gives Virgo the strength they need to face many challenges in life. Virgos can use their life experiences to teach others how to become more resilient.

Overcoming obstacles and challenging negative beliefs about themselves will help Virgos foster resiliency. When Virgos notice something about themselves that is holding them back or preventing happiness, they work extra hard to change it. Virgos seek perfection and go above and beyond to fix things that are broken. Learning to control their critical nature helps them become a happier person.

It is important for Virgos to focus on health and diet by ensuring that they eat nutritious foods, take vitamins, make time to exercise, and find time to relax. Virgos become stressed out easily and experience anxiety due to their high-strung nature, which can affect their ability to take care of themselves. It is important for Virgos to keep a structured daily routine when experiencing crisis or change.

Many Virgos have an amazing ability to express their feelings when communicating or writing. Journaling helps cultivate greater self-awareness. Sharing their deepest thoughts and feelings with those closest to them boosts resiliency. When Virgos admit that they need help and accept assistance from others, they transform relationships. Talking openly to friends and family helps Virgos overcome feelings of depression and anxiety. It is important for Virgos to remember that adjusting to change can be difficult and they shouldn't be too hard on themselves. Treating themselves with the same compassion and kindness that they give to others is part of their journey. Virgos need to remember they will make mistakes and that is okay, because no one is perfect all the time.

How to Support a Virgo

If a there is a Virgo in your life, show them that you truly care. Prove to them that they can trust you to be there. Offer them your help and practical support. They will never ask for help, so do practical things for them such as cleaning the house, dusting, doing the dishes, or taking the dog for a walk. They will appreciate it if you allow them to have their own routine and time to be alone. Spend quality time communicating with them when they want to talk. Make them laugh and help them let their hair down and relax.

Virgo Reflection Questions

- What helps you control obsessive thoughts?
- What helps you focus on and stick to your routine?

- Is there anything you need to heal?

- What personality traits help you become more resilient?

- How do you handle stress and anxiety?

Virgo Affirmations

- "My outlook is optimistic. My stress levels are low. My relationships are healthy."

- "My environment is clean. My spiritual connection is maintained. I replenish my physical body."

- "I nurture myself. I treat myself with the same care and attention that I give to others."

- "I prioritize my health by eating healthy food."

- "I release worry over things I can't control."

Virgo Self-Care Ideas

- Spend a day at the spa getting a massage and haircut.

- Make time to be alone so you can journal your thoughts and feelings.

- Spend time outdoors in nature. Go hiking or take a walk.

- Create three positive affirmations to recite daily.

- List three self-care techniques you find helpful and make time to do those things.

- Draw a flower with seven petals. Write down one new self-care activity you want to implement in each of the petals. Then hang the flower on the wall as a reminder. Try to do one new self-care activity every day until you've incorporated them into your routine.

THE SIXTH HOUSE

The importance of having a healthy physical body is crucial for human beings to survive. The type of work environment we have and whether or not it is stable, predictable, and healthy or unstable, toxic, and unhealthy can truly impact us psychologically, mentally, and physically. Having a routine is one of the most important things human beings can do to ensure a positive work environment and health are maintained. Some individuals thrive in an unstable work environment better than others, depending on which planets are placed here.

The sixth house is the house of structure, routine, health, and diet. All issues related to what we eat and put into our bodies, how much we exercise, and when and how we relieve stress are all sixth-house issues. Virgo is the sign known for perfectionism, worry, hypochondriac tendencies, and being health conscious, and Virgo rules this house. The type of work environment we thrive in and the type of relationships we have with coworkers are also ruled by the sixth house.

Looking at specific planet placements in the sixth house can also tell a lot about health and potential disease. For instance, if Pluto is in the sixth house, there is often vulnerability in the reproductive region and elimination system. Conditions like ovarian cysts, endometriosis, irritable bowel syndrome, colon problems, and stress-related illnesses can manifest in the physical body. The energy of the sixth house impacts our health even if we do not have specific planets placed there. It is important to look and see what sign is on the sixth house cusp to further investigate health vulnerabilities.

Another way sixth-house energy manifests in our lives is that it can cause obsessive-compulsive tendencies. The energy of this house can create a strong desire to do something a certain way regardless of the necessity for it. The energy of the sixth house can manifest in many different ways and in a variety of different scenarios. The important thing to remember is that this house has an impact on our daily life and physical health.

If you don't have planets in the sixth house, this not a negative thing. It simply means that your life lessons are not focused on this area of life. It is important to look at the sign on the sixth house cusp to see what energy impacts your health, diet, and day-to-day routine. For instance, if you have Virgo on the sixth house cusp, you need structure and control. You are a diligent worker. Completing tasks and organizing things comes naturally—but so does worry, anxiety, and a desire to feel in control of your work environment.

IF YOU HAVE PLANETS IN THE SIXTH HOUSE

Sixth-house people are hardworking, organized, and health conscious. You enjoy a stable routine. With planets here, helping others who are struggling comes easily to you. You are health conscious; watching what you eat and implementing exercise is a beneficial addition to your routine. You crave organization, reliability, and structure.

The sixth house rules the physical body and health, and people with sixth-house planets often have a sensitivity to the environment. As a child, you likely had health problems, seasonal and food allergies, or unexplained illnesses. Sixth-house people like controlling the environment and planning ahead;

controlling the things around you brings comfort. Planets here cause health consciousness, but try to avoid going to extremes. Balancing healthy eating behaviors and implementing a solid routine are important when planets are placed in the sixth house. Not getting enough sleep, exercise, or vitamins can increase stress levels. Do not let your perfectionist tendencies destroy your happiness.

Having planets in the sixth house creates a high-strung nature. You find it difficult to settle down and relax. As a person who resists change, it's important for things to run smoothly in an organized way. You might experience difficulties with coworkers; a stressful environment can affect your mood. Unstable emotions can affect your health and stress weakens your immune system, making you prone to sickness. When you find yourself in a work environment that becomes stressful, calling in sick more often is something you do to escape. Harmony, a well-balanced work environment, and communication with coworkers is needed.

Exploring New Age practices like essential oils, flower essences, herbs, acupuncture, and energy healing such as Reiki builds helping skills. There is an attraction to alternative healing professions and the medical field. Many individuals with sixth-house planets work in the medical field and take care of others in a hospital or clinical setting. Detached and stable during crisis situations, you provide others with a calm demeanor. Being of service is what you were born to do, but you need to be cautious about giving too much. Sixth-house planets can contribute to burnout and compassion fatigue. Making time to recover and recharge energy by taking breaks to nurture yourself is important.

The sixth house also rules small animals, so enjoyment comes from spending time with pets. Sometimes animals are preferred over people. Animals bring you comfort, reduce stress, and become a therapeutic tool.

Planets in the Sixth House

If you have one or more planets in the sixth house, read the corresponding sections for tips for transformation, healing, and resilience.

Sun in the Sixth House

You are a person who shines at work, but you can be preoccupied with health concerns. This placement creates blessings and difficulties regarding physical health. Remaining healthy and maintaining practical routines are important for managing self-care. This placement makes you strive for perfectionism in daily tasks, which can be exhausting. Because you push hard to achieve your goals, it is natural to feel a lot of stress. Accept that you don't have to do everything perfectly and that everyone makes mistakes.

The sun in the sixth house creates a dislike for change and the unexpected. Proper nutrition, organized work environments, and getting enough physical activity are important for your happiness. You are capable of great achievements, and being recognized for working hard boosts your self-esteem. With the sun here, nurturing and taking care of others comes naturally to you. You may be drawn to careers in the medical field such as nursing, social work, or dentistry.

Moon in the Sixth House

You are a caring person who needs an occupation where you can help others and be of service. Born with practical skills for taking care of others, you are happy cooking, doing laundry, organizing, and cleaning for your loved ones. You are happiest with a structured routine. Having a schedule and monotony brings comfort and security. If things change unexpectedly, your health can be affected, so learn how to handle stress.

The environment can impact your mood in positive and negative ways. The moon here shows the importance of taking care of your own emotional needs; prioritize your personal life and alone time. With this placement, it's easy to balance your emotions if you make an effort to nurture your overall health and well-being. Balancing the mind by meditating or journaling ensures happiness and good mental health.

Mercury in the Sixth House

You are an energetic person focused on pursuing work goals. As a clear and concise communicator, you can multitask and accomplish great things. Mercury is at home here, which helps encourage fruitful communication with coworkers. Communicating with your coworkers can inspire them to achieve greater success. Utilize your natural writing talents and organizational skills to make your work environment a better place. Jobs that are structured and organized are where you thrive; you have a strong attention to detail when completing complicated projects. This placement focuses energy on helping others in professions such as psychology, counseling, or teaching.

Venus in the Sixth House

You are a person who finds joy in routine tasks. Finding ways to make daily chores easy and enjoyable is your forte. With this placement, there is a tendency to eat sugary foods to cope with stress, so managing weight can be challenging. It is best to stick to a healthy, balanced diet and an exercise routine.

With this placement, work and pleasure go hand in hand. Your work environment needs to be peaceful and harmonious with a focus on career advancement. Activities such as modeling, acting, singing, or anything where you can express your feelings creates happiness. It is important for your overall well-being to create pleasant relationships with supportive coworkers. Sometimes this placement attracts romantic partners through work, travel, and conferences.

Mars in the Sixth House

You are a person who is driven to succeed at work. As a master delegator and leader, you're able to accomplish goals quickly. You are always getting a lot done, and most of your coworkers can't keep up with your high energy level. Being a part of a team and surrounding yourself with people that meet your high standards of work ethic, determination, and power is important. You like to take action in the work environment, which sometimes creates tension and conflict with coworkers. At times you are passionate, aggressive, and shrewd when it comes to getting what you want. Learn to compromise by allowing others to have what they want too; it is important to heal relationships with coworkers.

Learning to balance your work responsibilities and family is critical for your overall happiness. A high-intensity workout routine will help burn off anger, frustration, and irritability. Instead of focusing on self-centered goals, shift your focus to serving those in need.

Jupiter in the Sixth House

This placement is all about expansion and taking on big projects. Watch out for procrastination and being too easygoing; rushing around and doing things last minute can cause additional stress for you and your coworkers. The good thing about this placement is that you're lucky and blessed with positive energy when it comes to work. You are a person who has good luck with career opportunities and success; things always have a tendency to work out in your favor. You have a generous spirit, and helping coworkers and those who are suffering creates a sense of purpose.

Growth occurs when you become more prepared, organized, and structured. Be cautious about overindulgence in food and alcohol because this can affect your health. Incorporate movement daily, implement exciting activities, and travel as often as you can.

Saturn in the Sixth House

You are a person who has a serious personality and feels restricted by work. Serving others seems more like a duty or chore that has to be done rather than something that you want to do. Saturn in the sixth house might make you feel like you can never do enough and that no one is there for you when you need assistance. Feeling burdened is common with this placement, and your responsibilities can seem overwhelming.

Serious and responsible at heart, you are always working hard to get tasks done correctly. You need strict daily routines and like to control your environment. Heal karma with your coworkers by developing a more positive attitude. Repressing your emotions, having insecurities about your health, and anxiety about illness are all sixth-house issues. Combat stress by enjoying vacations, stepping away, taking breaks when needed, and learning to relax away from work.

Uranus in the Sixth House

This placement is difficult because it creates feelings of being trapped by the environment. Uranus in the sixth house likes to rebel against the status quo; efficiency can seem boring and restricting. You are a person who wants to break free from comfortable routines. It helps to come up with inventive and creative ways to solve problems and complete innovative tasks. Having open-minded coworkers and supervisors and a work environment where you are able to express your individuality is key. If you don't feel a sense of freedom and independence at work, you might rebel aggressively. Erratic behavior can damage relationships with colleagues. You may struggle with routine, and this can lead to stress-related illnesses. This is why it's crucial for your work environment to support your unique personality and ideas.

Neptune in the Sixth House

You are a compassionate person who sacrifices yourself to serve others. Giving your time, energy, and strength to others is what you do best. Feeling needed by others and knowing that you are making a difference in other people's lives brings you happiness.

You are sensitive to energy; this is heightened by Neptune in the sixth house. Absorbing other people's thoughts and emotions is common with this placement. Because of this, you may experience overwhelming feelings, especially if working with people who are suffering from illnesses. Avoiding conflict and escaping from challenging coworkers is a common coping mechanism. It is important to learn to develop boundaries to protect your energy and to take better care of yourself.

Replenishing your energy and balancing stress helps transform your unhealthy behaviors. If you do not address stress head on, you could suffer from physical illnesses that are mysterious and difficult to diagnose. With Neptune here, it is important to always get a second opinion when suffering from a medical diagnosis. You may have sensitivities to certain medications and foods. Take care of your health by implementing healthy habits and establishing a daily routine.

Pluto in the Sixth House

Pluto in the sixth house makes you intensely focused on work, and you accomplish a lot of tasks as a result of sheer discipline. You are a person who might experience power and control issues with coworkers. If you refuse to address issues in your work environment, your physical health can suffer. Make time to nurture and balance relationships with your coworkers by trying not to control other people. Building trusting relationships with coworkers creates growth and an awareness that others can be supportive of your goals.

You are blessed with strong recuperative and healing abilities and overcome illness quickly. It is important to implement healthy eating habits and self-care techniques into your daily routine. Express your true feelings instead of repressing them. This placement intensifies a need for change, growth, and transformation of daily routines.

LIBRA & THE SEVENTH HOUSE

Nickname: Libra the Peacemaker

Symbol: The scales

Sun Sign Dates: September 23–October 23

Ruler: Venus

Rules: The seventh house; the kidneys and lower back

Sign Type: Air, cardinal

Polar Opposite Sign: Aries

Tips for Healing: Learn to compromise, make decisions, experience partnership

Libra is a cardinal sign, which means Libras are initiators and like to come up with new ideas. As an air sign, they are intelligent, calm, and easygoing. Happiness comes from pursuing relationships with others and developing romantic bonds. Ruled by the planet Venus, Libras are attracted to things that involve fairness, justice, creativity, art, love, and beauty. An interesting fact is that they are the only zodiac sign not ruled by a living thing; the symbol that rules Libra is the scales of balance, which are made out of metal.

CHALLENGING ATTRIBUTES OF A LIBRA

Libra's scales are always tilting back and forth trying to find balance. When they become imbalanced and out of harmony, they can lose touch with their true thoughts and feelings. Indecisive by nature, they find it hard to make up their mind because they always see the validity of both sides in an argument.

It is difficult for people to truly get to know Libras because they often seem shy and reserved. Those closest to them feel they are not direct in expressing what they really want. Communication problems arise due to Libras' strong desire to avoid conflict and confrontation. A Libra's need for peace and harmony at all costs can create uncomfortable situations where they are forced to choose a side, and this is not easy. They grow more confident when they can share what they truly believe without fear of upsetting others. Learning to express their amazing ideas, thoughts, and feelings actually helps them find greater balance.

Positive Attributes of a Libra

Libras are known to be diplomatic, creative, romantic, and artistic. It is true that there are two sides to their personality: one artistic and one intellectual. Symbolized by the scales of balance, Libras are always trying to make decisions and balance their emotions. They are happiest when fighting for causes that they care about, and fighting for the underdog comes naturally to them.

Libras find equilibrium and contentment by doing the right thing and fighting for truth and fairness. They believe in justice, so they are drawn to careers such as law, criminal justice, and law enforcement.

Many Libras have amazing negotiating skills and are able to help others that are experiencing conflict. They are natural peacemakers, and their calm nature helps stabilize those around them. Utilizing their natural ability to communicate with others helps model ways to express feelings openly. This helps strengthen relationships and bonds with family members. Being a role model and showing others how to compromise is Libra's natural gift. Strong relationships with others increase a Libra's ability to overcome difficulties. Being able to mediate with people in times of crisis is a gift that can be used to overcome many obstacles. Libras do best when they embrace conflict, make decisions, face difficult conversations, and nurture their relationships.

Relationships with a Libra

Naturally beautiful and attractive, many people are drawn into a Libra's inner circle. Libras often rely on their partners or friends to make decisions for them because they are indecisive. They crave peace and harmony in all areas of life, so they make an effort to avoid conflict and confrontation. Libras must learn to accept the fact that pleasing everyone all the time is impossible; this is an important lesson.

One of a Libra's biggest flaws is that they tend to go along with others and not express what they truly want. Libras try not to upset anyone and resist taking sides by staying in the middle. Many people like to share their personal problems with Libras, and sometimes they are forced to mediate conflicts. Because they are natural peacemakers, they help their friends work through disagreements. It is common for them to change the subject during intense arguments, and they may withdraw or physically leave social situations that are uncomfortable.

It makes sense that the seventh house is ruled by Libra. The descendant, also known as the seventh house cusp or relationship area, is ruled by Libra, making marriage and partnerships a primary focus for Libras. Finding a soul mate, lover, or business partner is important for Libras because being alone does not bring them happiness—being in love does. More than any other sign, Libras need to find love and someone they can depend on. Without a trustworthy, stable partner, they can wither and struggle with life. Making time to seek a relationship with another person brings them stability. Because they are naturally charming, attracting romantic partners comes easily for Libras. Once they have found a partner, Libras enjoy affection and quality time in their relationships. It is important for them to find a trustworthy partner who helps them feel capable of conquering any limitation. A major lesson Libra has to learn is to be more cautious about sacrificing their own needs for the needs of their partners.

Libra Tips for Transformation

Relationships can be a challenge for Libras even though they crave love. On one hand, they truly desire having someone to love, and on the other hand, they avoid people due to fears of acceptance. Sacrificing their own feelings for others comes naturally, so allowing themselves to be honest, confident, direct, and expressive will foster transformation.

Make Your Own Decisions

Libras are known for not taking action right away because they prefer to think about all sides of an issue. They are intelligent and can see both the positive and negative sides in all situations. Because of this indecisiveness, Libras often rely on others to make hard decisions for them. When Libras step out of their comfort zone by making their own decisions and choosing a specific path, they can transform. They gain confidence and strength when they make difficult choices instead of withdrawing.

Find Balance

When a Libra makes time to balance their thoughts and feelings, their life transforms. Libras have to find creative ways to establish equilibrium in life. Experiencing emotional highs and lows is common, and stress triggers imbalance. Recognizing when they are feeling stressed will help Libras take time to ground themselves.

Being an air sign blesses Libras with both a creative and intellectual personality. Many are talented at math, science, and technology and also are gifted at drawing, painting, playing music, or writing. It's important for Libras to express their creative gifts. It can be hard for Libra to pick one talent to focus on.

Express Your Thoughts and Feelings

Overcoming passive tendencies is important because other people might try to take advantage of them. It is common to see Libras withdrawing when disagreements come up with friends, family, and coworkers; they resist conflict at all costs. There are times when Libras are forced into the middle of arguments as the peacemaker, giving advice and breaking up disagreements. Transformation comes when Libras are assertive, choose a side, and stick to it.

Libras benefit when they realize that challenges and conflicts help create growth. Life can be boring if we never feel angry or upset. Libras need to remember that they are human and have every right to feel unpleasant emotions. They need to learn how to stand up for themselves when necessary, step out of their comfort zone, and speak the truth regardless of what others think.

LIBRA TIPS FOR HEALING

Libras heal by vocalizing their feelings and by allowing themselves to partner with others. It is easy to put themselves in another person's shoes and understand why others feel the way they do. Healing occurs when they allow compromise with others and work out disagreements. Finding stable, peaceful, and loving relationships is important to their overall health and well-being. Developing healthy relationships that allow an equal amount of give and take is important for maintaining happiness. Sometimes struggles happen in life when they are unable to find the right person to love.

Find Healthy Partnership

More than any other sign, it's important for Libras to have comforting, harmonious, and supportive relationships. Libras can experience depression, loneliness, and isolation if they do not have other people surrounding them. At some point in their life, they may become involved in unhealthy relationships simply because they were lonely; these relationships then lead to pain, heartache, and difficulty. Moving forward and healing any past relationship wounds is important. When Libras heal the past, it will be easier to open up and trust others again.

Work on Indecisiveness

Finding a way to balance indecisiveness and avoidant behaviors will bring healing. Sometimes it is uncomfortable to deal with conflict, so hiding is Libra's second nature. They need to realize and accept that feeling angry is normal because it is a natural human emotion. Learning how to accept their feelings, express unpleasant emotions, and communicate their thoughts creates stronger relationships and leads to growth.

Manage Conflict

Libras need to allow themselves to experience conflict with others and face it head on. They will begin to realize that it is normal to disagree with others and that relationships can still stay intact through disagreements. Compromising and discussing differences of opinions in an open and honest way instead of running away from conflict helps facilitate healing.

Control Stress Levels

A Libra's vulnerable area is the lower back and kidneys. Excessive stress can cause lower back pain and spasms. Kidney infections and stones are common if stress levels are not balanced. It is important for Libras to drink enough fluids throughout the day and while traveling to avoid dehydration. Finding balance in all areas of life helps nourish the body and control stress levels. Spending time reading, learning, or expressing artistic abilities will bring greater healing.

LIBRA RESILIENCY

Libras are relationship seekers. They want to be in love. Finding someone to spend their life with is often on the forefront of their mind. Libras need to let go of insecurities about never finding the right partner; they must accept that there will be times when they are single and alone, which is not easy for them. Overcoming feelings of loneliness when they don't have someone to love can be challenging. Libras find resilience when they move forward in life—with or without a partner by their side.

Libras are successful in relationships because of their natural ability to compromise and see other people's points of view. Putting their partner's needs first and sacrificing their feelings for others are things Libras need to learn how to balance. Speaking up for their own needs helps increase self-reliance and assertiveness.

HOW TO SUPPORT A LIBRA

If there is a Libra in your life, spend quality time together. Do something romantic for them. Surprise them with gifts and be affectionate. Encourage them to communicate, and be a good listener. Accept that they might be quiet at times. Discuss your concerns with them openly and honestly. Avoid conflict and respect their need for peace and harmony. Allow them to spend time with other people if they need to. Encourage them to pursue their artistic interests.

LIBRA REFLECTION QUESTIONS

- How do you handle conflict?
- What type of relationship partner are you attracted to?
- Is there anything you need to heal?
- What personality traits help you become more resilient?
- How do you handle stress and anxiety?

LIBRA AFFIRMATIONS

- "I am happiest when I prioritize my own needs."
- "I need time to recharge. I know it is healthy for me to spend time on my own."
- "I have so much love in my life. I value my partnerships."
- "I am creative. I am talented. I embrace my artistic side."

LIBRA SELF-CARE IDEAS

- Allow yourself to spend time alone to recharge.
- Spend time reading and studying something new.
- Express your creative side by drawing, painting, or writing
- Create three positive affirmations to recite daily.

- List three self-care techniques you find helpful and make time to do those things.

- Draw a flower with seven petals. Write down one new self-care activity you want to implement in each of the petals. Then hang the flower on the wall as a reminder. Try to do one new self-care activity every day until you've incorporated them into your routine.

THE SEVENTH HOUSE

The seventh house represents our partner and our relationships with significant others. The type of partnership you will have can be understood by looking at the planets in the seventh house or the sign that is on the descendant. The sign on the cusp of the seventh house will reveal the personality traits of your ideal partner. For example, if you have Virgo on the descendant, you will benefit from having a partner who is organized, reliable, and helpful. Not only does the seventh house represent intimate relationships in our lives, it also shows the possibility of business partnerships. Most people enjoy intimacy and having romantic relationships with others; seventh-house people are known to focus on having companionship and avoid being alone.

As human beings, having companionship is important for our psychological well-being. We need others around us to cuddle, talk with, and count on. The seventh house is an important area of life where we can let our hair down, cry and express our emotions, and open up about things we might not readily share with others. If we are lucky, we find true happiness by finding the perfect partner that encourages us, motivates us, and stands by us.

Certain planets that fall in the seventh house can have a significant impact on relationship development, partner choices, and relationship satisfaction. It is crucial to look at the seventh house to determine what type of lessons are meant to be learned. I had a client who had the moon placed in the seventh house, and she told me she felt empty without a partner. She had anxiety whenever she was alone and needed to have a relationship partner to experience fulfillment. Her emotional security was connected to having a partner and being in an intimate relationship.

Certain planet placements in the seventh house can indicate positive karma from forming business partnerships; others can indicate a need for caution. For instance, someone with Uranus placed in the seventh house would be advised not to partner with others in business due to unexpected, unforeseen changes with their partners. As for marriage, these individuals would be advised to wait and truly get to know someone because this placement can attract unstable or unreliable people.

If you don't have planets in the seventh house, this simply means there will be no significant life lessons related to marriage, partnership, and relationships. It does not mean that you will not have relationships or have bad luck with love. You will need to look at the sign on the cusp of the seventh house to understand what you need in relationships and the type of partners that you attract. For instance, if Scorpio is on the seventh house cusp, you will be secretive, intense, possessive, and private when you are in relationships. It will take time for you to fully trust your partner enough to be vulnerable.

If You Have Planets in the Seventh House

When planets are in the seventh house, there is value in having relationships. Someone who feels a strong urge to bond with another human being usually has seventh-house planets. Having intimate relationships and learning to compromise will be a primary focus in your life. You do not like dating around and prefer to have stable, long-term relationships and commitment. The biggest lesson you are learning is that your partner can't always come first. Balancing your own needs in relationships is an important lesson of this house. Karma in relationships is common with planets in the seventh house; there could be great joy or great pain.

You learn about yourself through partnerships because you grow more as a person when loving others. Other people serve as a mirror and show what areas of your life need to change. Marriage and commitment are important areas of focus, and being single is more difficult for you than for people who do not have planets in the seventh house. If you do not have a committed loving relationship, then you spend most of your time with close friends doing something creative and fun.

You need healthy relationships in your life or you can become depressed and uncomfortable. It can be difficult for you to be happy without a love interest. Sometimes planets here indicate marriage at a young age. Rushing into marriage can cause heartache and regrets later on in life; it is best to take time to get to know others before making lasting commitments. When planets are in the seventh house, it is crucial that great care be taken to ensure marriage to someone healthy and supportive occurs. Attracting the wrong partners can have devastating effects on life satisfaction, personal happiness, and health. It is difficult for you to function in other areas of life when your intimate relationships are not harmonious.

Losing relationships can be extremely painful for seventh-house people because you get attached easily. Letting people go and allowing connections with new people can be difficult for you. Sometimes you are able to stay friends with others after a break up. Balance is key for you; you must learn to be comfortable being alone. There will be times when you won't have people around to rely on, and this is a great lesson in self-reliance.

Planets in the seventh house can create codependent behaviors. Others in your life might not understand your intense need to be in a relationship. Be careful not to ignore your friends and family when you are in a relationship. Don't forget there is nothing more important than finding contentment and happiness on your own.

Planets in the Seventh House

If you have one or more planets in the seventh house, read the corresponding section for tips for transformation, healing, and resilience.

Sun in the Seventh House

You are a person who craves relationships with people. One-on-one interaction is where you shine and express yourself best. Excellent negotiation skills makes it easy to get what you want from others. You have a knack for knowing what people want and being able to give it to them. Complimentary toward others, your charm helps manipulate situations in your own favor.

Attracting relationships happens easily with this placement. Finding happiness with a marriage partner will bring financial and emotional benefits. Business partnerships can also bring good luck and success. With this placement it's important to control fears of being alone.

Moon in the Seventh House

You are a person who finds emotional stability via your relationships. You are talented at compromising and communicating with others, and partnering for a common goal brings emotional comfort. Because you are always taking care of others, you have an expectation that others will take care of your emotional needs. Your emotional happiness can be impacted by the relationships in your life. Conflict in relationships causes you intense stress and anxiety. Sociable and charming, it's important to remember that feelings are changeable in love relationships. Floating from relationship to relationship is common with this placement. You are attracted to and interested in many different people who satisfy your interests. It is important to learn to balance relationship needs with personal responsibilities. Learn to do things on your own and get comfortable listening to your inner feelings.

Mercury in the Seventh House

You are a person who is lucky in relationships because of an easygoing, detached approach. An excellent communicator, you can express your thoughts easily with romantic partners. You enjoy conversation and discussing many different intellectually stimulating topics. It is important to commit to partners who are intelligent and mentally challenging to avoid boredom. Learn to control obsessing about relationships and stop overanalyzing emotions. Utilize your natural skills as a peacemaker to solve problems in relationships.

Venus in the Seventh House

You enjoy finding love and having intimate relationships. Peace-loving by nature, you often ignore negative qualities in others and focus on the positive aspects of relationships. Having a charming, attractive presence that is tender and affectionate attracts people. It is important with this placement to commit to someone and build a life together. You are calm, stable, loving, and affectionate, and others are lucky to have you in their life. Surrounding yourself with positive people brings happiness; stay away from aggressive or toxic people. Express your values and sense of fairness in all relationships. Develop skills in negotiation, marketing, and sales because these skills can bring success in business partnerships.

Mars in the Seventh House

You are a person who experiences power struggles in relationships. Strong-willed and assertive, controlling others causes conflict in your life. Fighting and arguing with partners happens when you don't get what you want or feel let down by others. You have a passionate drive to bond with someone, and this placement attracts confident, strong-willed partners. Stop trying to control partners and learn to tame your jealous streak. With Mars here it is important to balance your demanding, domineering nature with loved ones by learning patience. By controlling your anger, you avoid pushing away people that you care about. Mars here is focused on getting its own needs met, but relationships need compromise. This placement shows karmic learning related to relationships. Focus on the needs of others.

Jupiter in the Seventh House

You have a positive and giving nature in relationships. Avoid toxic and negative people. Feeling free is very important in your partnerships. Jupiter here needs the ability to roam, move, and explore in relationships. It is crucial to make time for travel and vacations with your partner. Known to be generous and giving, doing things for your partner brings you happiness. Partnering brings good luck abundance and financial blessings.

It can be difficult for you to remain happy with a partner, and at least two marriages are often seen with this placement. Because you are light-hearted and restless, be careful not to lose those closest to you due to neglecting them. Balance fears and avoid rebelling from committed relationships.

Saturn in the Seventh House

You are a person who takes relationships very seriously. You value commitment in relationships and are not someone who seeks multiple partners. Fears of being trapped in relationships are common with this placement. Unusually high expectations that are self-imposed can block intimacy. Focus on developing a positive attitude and learn to have more fun in relationships. Attracting partners who are older and marrying later in life are beneficial, although many with this placement marry at a young age and have difficulties ending relationships. Resist the urge to control your partners. Learning to trust and forgive others are karmic lessons of this placement. Pick partners for love, not for security reasons.

Uranus in the Seventh House

You are a person who needs a lot of freedom and friendship in relationships. Feeling trapped by committed relationships is a common feeling with this placement. Do not suppress your frustrations or ignore your feelings because it can lead to rebelling unexpectedly. If you feel suffocated or trapped, you will spark change and end relationships abruptly. It is important for you to overcome boredom and control your restless nature. Many with this placement experience divorce or gravitate toward unique partnerships, such as open relationships.

Unexpected things will happen in your love life and business partnerships with Uranus placed here. Be cautious when forming business partnerships because there can be unexpected losses. Being attracted to unusual and eccentric people is common. This placement shows a dislike for emotional displays of affection; you prefer a detached approach.

Neptune in the Seventh House

You are a person who values spirituality and kindness in relationships. A lack of boundaries can be an issue that affects trust and intimacy. Communication with partners can be distorted and involve misunderstandings with Neptune placed here. Born with an extremely romantic nature, seeking a spiritual soul mate is a priority of yours. Make sure to see the good and bad in relationship partners and avoid being overly idealistic. It is important to take off the rose-colored glasses and see people clearly to avoid emotional pain. Sacrificing what you truly want for others is common with this placement. Be cautious and don't allow others to take advantage of your kindness.

This placement creates a deep emotional nature and intensified compassion and empathy. Expressing love and receiving love in return is important for your happiness. Extremely romantic and giving, you love helping others who have problems. When you feel needed, you feel content. Overcome the desire to escape real-world responsibilities by becoming dependent on a partner. Attracting healthy, stable, supportive, and spiritual partners who can support your needs is key to finding happiness. It is important to end unhealthy relationships once and for all.

Pluto in the Seventh House

You are a deep person who needs intensity in relationships. On one hand you deeply want to connect with others, but you are also suspicious of people's motives. Perceptive and intuitive, seeing fakeness and lies comes easily with Pluto placed here. You are often slow to trust or commit to others because you need time to make sure your partner's words and actions match. A lesson of this placement is learning to trust others and become more vulnerable.

With Pluto here, power and control issues are common in relationships. Be cautious of marrying someone who is abusive, controlling, or aggressive. There might be negative relationship experiences where you felt abused and mistreated. Intensity in relationships can attract abusive or unhealthy people, and it's important to heal your wounds involving partnerships. It is recommended to marry later in life. Building greater self-awareness and understanding how to control your jealous and possessive nature improves partnerships.

Scorpio & the Eighth House

Nickname: Scorpio the Secretive One

Symbol: The scorpion

Sun Sign Dates: October 24–November 21

Ruler: Pluto

Rules: The eighth house; the sexual organs and elimination system

Sign Type: Water, fixed

Polar Opposite Sign: Taurus

Tips for Healing: Find forgiveness, express emotions, trust others

Scorpio is a fixed sign, which means Scorpios are practical, determined, and strong-willed. Born with an insightful, perceptive, and intense personality, this enhances their ability to know what is happening around them. Scorpio is ruled by the water element, so Scorpios experience intense emotions and intuitive abilities. At first glance they may appear reserved, observant, and secretive. Scorpios are known to avoid small talk and dislike anything superficial.

CHALLENGING ATTRIBUTES OF A SCORPIO

Scorpios are the most difficult people to get to know because they are private and distrust others. It takes them a long time to open up and become vulnerable. Appearing weak is not appealing to them, and neither is having to discuss emotions, struggles, or problems with others. A common trait for Scorpios is feeling very lonely but preferring to fight through life's challenges on their own, never asking for help.

Known for having a powerful energy and magnetism, many people can feel their intense emotions. Scorpios can be focused and calculating when it comes to getting what they want. They are competitive with others and experience emotional extremes; they want all or nothing in relationships. Not being prepared is difficult for Scorpios, and this makes them want to control everything. It is common for Scorpios to experience arguments and conflicts with others due to their need for power.

POSITIVE ATTRIBUTES OF A SCORPIO

Born with natural healing abilities, enjoyment can be found in helping others solve complex emotional problems. Scorpios are great listeners, and others frequently confess all their secrets to them. As a very self-aware individual who is psychologically gifted, helping others heal comes naturally for a Scorpio. They understand pain, sadness, and loss more than any other sign. Scorpios make great therapists, psychiatrists, business owners, supervisors, investigators, and detectives because they see through facades, fakeness, and lies. They are known to have deep, penetrating eyes—it's like they see right through others. Scorpios have an inborn intuition and psychic awareness of what is truly happening with others and in the environment, but they do not like others to analyze them because they value their privacy above all else.

Born with psychic abilities, they can extract dark secrets from others. It's hard to hide anything from them. This ability comes from the fact that Scorpio is the ruler of the eighth house in the birth chart.

Scorpios enjoy digging into the harsh realities of life and are not afraid to discuss death and sexuality. Exploring taboo issues that most people try to pretend do not exist intrigues them. The issue of death impacts them personally from a young age. Due to personal experiences with loss, Scorpios have a deep awareness of the meaning of life. They may tell death-related jokes or talk about death in social situations while everyone around them feels uncomfortable. They are drawn to subjects like astrology, tarot, magic, and mysticism. Many like to research things that are deep, psychological, and transformative. Even if Scorpios do not study occult subjects, they probably are open-minded and curious. Many Scorpios believe in supernatural phenomena. However, they will probably never admit it due to their secretive nature.

Repressing and hiding emotions is common for Scorpios; they are extremely cautious people who question everyone's motives. It is not a bad thing to wait to make sure that individuals are worthy enough to be trusted. Deep life challenges are something they think about and try to prepare for. Scorpios like to be ready for change and have an instinctual need to control any future outcomes that might occur.

RELATIONSHIPS WITH A SCORPIO

Scorpios are known for their sexual passion and possess a magnetism that is undeniable, drawing individuals into their web. Scorpios attract others because they are mysterious. Some people are not comfortable with Scorpios because they can make others feel vulnerable with their silent treatment. Other people perceive them as secretive and someone who can withhold love and information.

When Scorpios are in a relationship, they tend to be possessive and are considered a jealous lover. They are known for getting others to tell them their secrets, but they will put a wall up and refuse to share their own secrets. Communication is difficult for many Scorpios. Naturally private, it's difficult for them to share personal information. They are known to withhold affection, information, and communication when they are upset with others. When they feel slighted, they are known to cut people off, walk away, and never look back. Betrayal is the one thing Scorpio can't forgive. They value commitment, loyalty, and honesty in all their relationships. They are intuitive, and they see through people easily. Superficiality and fakeness will turn them off. Scorpios need loyalty, sexual intimacy, and depth in relationships. The greatest challenge for Scorpios is to learn how to trust others.

Scorpio Tips for Transformation

Scorpios transform when they are able to fully trust others. They need to embrace the fact that they don't have to do everything on their own or struggle in silence. When Scorpios shut other people out and refuse to discuss their problems with close friends, they become more isolated.

Practice Forgiveness

Opening up to others can be difficult for a Scorpio. Once betrayed, it is very difficult for them to forgive and forget. Giving the silent treatment and never speaking to people again are defense mechanisms used for protection. Finding ways to forgive will help Scorpio transform and become more compassionate, caring, and understanding.

Embrace Your Inner Strength

Scorpio is associated with everything that has to do with transformation, rebirth, and growth. They should have an easier time moving forward in life than other signs. Adapting and changing how they feel about past injustices is something that occurs naturally. Scorpios are strong and bury unpleasant emotions so they can continue to survive. When life tests Scorpio, their inner strength pushes them toward adapting and overcoming despite difficulties.

Allow Vulnerability

Scorpios transform when they allow themselves to be more vulnerable. Being vulnerable does not make them weak; it actually makes it easier for loved ones to help them and communicate more openly. A Scorpio's secretiveness can prevent others from sharing honest and truthful emotions. If a Scorpio opens up and shares emotions with those they care about, their relationships will improve.

Cut Unhealthy Ties
Scorpios are known to cut people off and out of their life after the slightest disagreement. They do not find it easy to give others second chances. Letting go of unhealthy relationships and abusive people brings strength. Transformation comes easily for a Scorpio because of their ability to accept change. Scorpios move on, hiding memories in a secret filing cabinet in their heart.

SCORPIO TIPS FOR HEALING
Scorpios struggle with power and control issues. Being secretive is a way for Scorpio to protect themselves, but this behavior can make them feel lonely. The walls they have built up around themselves keep those closest to them at a distance.

Trust Others
Scorpios' personal healing comes from allowing themselves to be more trusting of others. In order for them to heal relationships and past wounds, they have to make extra effort to allow others into their private world. Trusting others and discussing private feelings and concerns will help them feel lighter and happier. Instead of repressing negative feelings, they need to release them to benefit their health. Letting things go and trusting life will help them release burdens.

Release the Past
To truly heal, Scorpios need to release dark emotions such as anger and jealousy as well as feelings of revenge. Scorpios need to learn that forgiveness does not mean what happened was not

hurtful, and just because they forgave someone does not mean they have to allow that person back into their life. Moving forward by cutting ties with the past helps Scorpio heal and accept their journey moving forward.

Experience Intimacy

Merging with a partner physically, emotionally, spiritually, and sexually helps Scorpios find greater intimacy. This requires them to be truly open and share parts of themselves that can be uncomfortable. Scorpios have to realize that people deserve a chance to prove themselves because everyone is different. Once Scorpios allow themselves to be more open and expressive, true healing can happen in their life.

Release Control

Scorpios can be possessive and overbearing. They may expect a lot from their loved ones. The more they try to control other people, the more likely they are to lose them. It is important for Scorpios to show they care by allowing others the freedom to be themselves. Life is full of change, and Scorpios can't control another person's behaviors or actions. Scorpios need to trust the process and accept the fact that they can't always predict the future. Their greatest strength can be found by releasing control and adapting to change.

Feel Your Emotions

When Scorpios don't handle stress, their body experiences illness. Health problems are often caused by repressing emotions, holding on to past hurts, and refusing to forgive. Scorpios are prone to problems with the reproductive system and elimination system. Problems affecting the sexual organs such as the ovaries, cervix, or uterus are common. Refusing to release intense emotions such as anger can be associated with cancer, constipation, irritable bowel syndrome, or colon problems. Finding positive ways to handle and balance their inner emotions will help improve overall health.

SCORPIO RESILIENCY

Scorpios can overcome many obstacles with their determination and courage. A survivor at heart, they find the inner strength to rise up again after many challenges. Embracing change by utilizing their powerful energy within is a gift. Resiliency is a natural ability that exists within, and this is why Scorpios are associated with the phoenix. They have the strength to rise from the ashes, reborn as a completely different person. Nothing keeps them down for long; they do not give up easily.

Scorpio is also known as the scorpion; they have a tail that stings and wounds when threatened. They know how to protect themselves and others. Their protective mechanism allows them to handle toxic people by having strong boundaries. They transform dangerous situations for survival. Becoming a stronger person occurs naturally after disappointment and pain. It blesses Scorpios with wisdom and life experience. Scorpios go through many transformative periods in their life, and upon reflection, they often realize they are not the same person they used to be.

Scorpios are always intuitively aware that life can change in the blink of an eye. Having this foresight and perceptive vision is what helps them prepare for the future. Blessed with a strong intuition and inner knowing, Scorpios often predict what is coming into their life. It's hard for them to be caught off guard because they always calculate the risks. Scorpios can cut off emotion when they need to, which helps them overcome heartache, betrayal, and mistreatment. This personality trait is the very thing that helps Scorpio develop resilience and bounce back when life knocks them down.

Helping others when they are struggling strengthens a Scorpio's ability to heal themselves. Born with the power of regeneration, they are the natural healers and psychologists of the zodiac.

How to Support a Scorpio

If there is a Scorpio in your life, grow with them and prove that you are a loyal person. Don't try to force them to open up and share feelings when they are not ready. Accept that they dislike small talk. Communicate your feelings directly and honestly with them at all times. Allow them to feel safe in your presence. Be reliable and stable so they will begin to trust you. Say what you mean and have your actions match your words. Show vulnerability and allow them to see your sensitive side. Encourage them to spend time alone when they need it.

Scorpio Reflection Questions

- Is there anyone you are angry with and need to forgive?
- How do you work on trusting others?
- Is there anything you need to heal?
- What personality traits make you more resilient?
- How do you handle stress and anxiety?

Scorpio Affirmations

- "I listen to my intuition and to my body. I heal myself before I heal others."

- "I believe everything happens for a reason. Conflict is a teacher, and I listen to its lessons."

- "I love myself unconditionally. I have everything I need to succeed within me."

- "Everyone in my life wants the best for me. I trust my inner circle will offer me support when I need it."

Scorpio Self-Care Ideas

- Make time to have privacy. Recharge by withdrawing socially.

- Spend time by the ocean or near a body of water.

- Exercise to release your intense emotions.

- Create three positive affirmations to recite daily.

- List three self-care techniques you find helpful and make time to do those things.

- Draw a flower with seven petals. Write down one new self-care activity you want to implement in each of the petals. Then hang the flower on the wall as a reminder. Try to do one new self-care activity every day until you've incorporated them into your routine.

THE EIGHTH HOUSE

At some point in our lives, we will all be faced with the death of someone we love. Some of us are shielded from this loss, and others experience it tragically at a young age. Losing someone we love is hard to understand, and many people do not even know how to talk about it. There are many taboo things in the world that we are taught not to talk about, and all of those issues fall within the eighth house; issues such as sacrifice, rebirth, sexuality, metaphysical topics, inheritances, other people's resources, secrets, and healing are all influenced by planets in the eighth house. Those things that we find difficult to think about or talk about because they are intense or uncomfortable—such as child abuse, sexual assault, murder, the death of our most cherished loved ones, and unexplained things like ghosts and aliens—are all eighth-house topics. It is no wonder that the secretive sign Scorpio rules the eighth house.

When I think about the eighth house, the first word that comes to my mind is *energy*. I think about the subtle energy that surrounds our physical bodies, known as *chi* or *prana*, and how this life force energy can be used to heal others. When planets are in the eighth house, there is a heightened sensitivity to these energies. Eighth-house people see others clearly and with brutal honesty. What others show on the outside is insignificant because eighth-house people can zone in on their true energy, emotions, and thoughts. However, this ability can make eighth-house people feel very alone. A deep feeling of loneliness can be associated with eighth-house planets.

If you don't have planets in the eighth house, this not a bad thing. You will want to look at the sign on the cusp of the eighth house to see what energy impacts your life. For instance, if Aries is on the eighth house cusp, you are naturally resilient when faced with difficult life experiences. Death of a loved one, betrayal, depression, and loss will be faced head on with confidence. You overcome many obstacles because you are self-motivated, strong, and have a desire to focus on the future.

If You Have Planets in the Eighth House

When there are planets here, there is usually the experience of losing a loved one at a young age, such as a parent, friend, or sibling. This house forces a deep awareness of the fragility of life. At a young age, you may have realized that people die and things change as you grappled with your own mortality.

The energy of the eighth house creates transformative paranormal experiences that you can't explain, usually starting in childhood. You have natural psychic abilities, an ability to dream about the future, and know what others are thinking and feeling. Embracing your spiritual gifts is important. The true lesson of this house is to realize that death is just an illusion and a transition.

Experiencing trauma involving sexuality and intimacy is a common eighth-house experience. The secrets you keep are often dark, powerful, and mysterious. Even those closest to you are often unaware of the hidden inner strength you possess. You tend to hide behind the scenes, never sharing the painful experiences you have lived through because you keep them locked deep inside. You are a survivor, but you often suffer in silence because burdening others with your problems is terrifying. It is hard for you to trust people enough to open up and allow vulnerability. You need to learn how to forgive. With time, you will be able to truly forgive those who have hurt you.

When planets are in the eighth house, helping others process deep emotions comes easily. Planets here make you a natural psychologist because you were born with empathy, compassion, and wisdom. Using your healing abilities to help others is an eighth-house lesson. You may be attracted to energy healing such as Reiki. You are good in crisis situations and often take charge, ensuring everyone is taken care of. Embracing change and thriving in crisis is an eighth-house gift. You were born to be a true healer who helps the wounded and those who have no one else. That's why people with planets in the eighth house are often called wounded healers.

Eighth-house people rise from the ashes and overcome things that most normal people would struggle to move on from. Early in life you learned to depend on yourself and no one else. You might get knocked down, but you always get back up. You are naturally resilient because you have survived difficult experiences. You might hit rock bottom, feel depressed, and struggle to get out of bed each day; these feelings could last for months before the voice inside says, "Get up." This voice is the voice of resiliency. You have to rise up stronger because the world needs your expertise. Stand up, dust off all the pain, and walk away from it. You have an ability to heal and cleanse your body, which is one of your greatest gifts. Adversity helps you bounce back stronger and become even more resilient. Transformation comes when you take all those memories, emotions, and painful experiences and morph into an entirely new person. The eighth-house energy of Scorpio and Pluto helps you ignite great regenerative energy.

With planets here, you are meant to rise like a phoenix out of the ashes. Emotional deaths, psychological deaths, and symbolic deaths transform who you are. It is important to release old pain and trauma. You are meant to be a beacon of hope for those who are hopeless. You are on earth to help people overcome the most difficult life circumstances and, through that process, you also heal yourself.

You may benefit from other people's resources. Many times, planets in the eighth house signify inheritance. You may inherit money, property, or land from loved ones who have passed on. Inheritance is not always money or land; you could also inherit psychic abilities or spiritual gifts passed on from someone in the family such as your parents, grandparents, aunts, or siblings.

Planets in the Eighth House

If you have one or more planets in the eighth house, read the corresponding section for tips for transformation, healing, and resilience.

Sun in the Eighth House

You are a person with a strong, powerful, and intense presence. Private and secretive at heart, you focus on hiding your true nature. This placement blesses you with a powerful intuition, psychic experiences, dreams, and empathic abilities. You were naturally gifted with healing energy. People with unhealed wounds are drawn to your magnetic personality and like to tell you their secrets. This placement makes you an excellent psychologist, detective, investigator, financial advisor, or mortician.

With the sun here, death of a loved one—such as the father or someone close—is a common experience. It is important to always embrace change whether it is positive or negative. Let change revamp your identity, personality, and appearance. Allow yourself to transform and emerge as a stronger version of yourself. Recover and recoup energy by withdrawing and spending time alone. Because you are fascinated by the mysteries of life, allow time to investigate occult subjects such as astrology, mysticism, death, and spirituality.

Moon in the Eighth House

You are a person who feels the pain of others and takes intimate relationships very seriously. Born with a very emotional, passionate, and sensitive nature, you absorb subtle energies in the environment. This placement makes you highly empathic, so it is important to learn how to protect your energy. Feeling other people's pain and suffering can affect you greatly, in both positive and negative ways. Helping others and listening to their problems comes naturally to you. You would make an excellent therapist because of your nurturing, healing presence.

Experiencing wounds involving intimacy, trust, and sexuality is common with the moon here. Secretive by nature, you often hide your true feelings from others. Repressing feelings and emotions is common due to a fear of being hurt. Sometimes you feel emotionally victimized by those you trust. Letting go of heavy burdens and finding peace is the goal of this placement. It is important not to expect relationship partners to fulfill all your needs; life gets better when you learn to compromise. Bonding with others emotionally, mentally, and physically is important for true happiness. Trust your intuition, feelings, and instincts because they are often right.

Mercury in the Eighth House

Because you are secretive by nature, you don't readily communicate, and you keep your thoughts private. But you are a person who needs deep communication in intimate relationships. Sharing your deepest, darkest thoughts with others helps process emotions. Communicate honestly with others and learn to build trust. Mentally connecting with people whom you can discuss metaphysical and occult subjects with is inspiring. Thinking about death and your own mortality is common with Mercury placed here.

You possess a sharp and perceptive mind, which makes it easy for you to read other people's thoughts. With this placement, there is an interest in research and detective work because of your ability to find answers to problems.

Venus in the Eighth House

People are attracted to your beauty and passionate energy. You are a person who finds pleasure in intimate relationships. Secretive and private, hiding your feelings from others is second nature. Developing healthy sexual relationships is important so you can express your desires and passion. Benefits come from having a partner, and marrying someone financially successful is common with this placement.

With Venus here, your loving nature is deep, possessive, and intense. Having Venus in the eighth house alleviates the heaviness of normal eighth-house energy. You are extremely kind, deep, and understanding, and learning how to forgive comes easier to you than other people with eighth-house placements.

Mars in the Eighth House

You are ambitious and assertive. Your relationships are intense, and your strong sex drive needs to be balanced. Getting your own needs met is important, but you can't expect partners to do everything you want. Try to avoid turbulent relationship conflicts and power struggles; power and control issues can affect intimate relationships when Mars is in the eighth house. Learning to control your intense desires and emotional needs will bring greater harmony to your relationships.

You are often involved in conflict due to your passionate personality. Be conscious of repressing your anger and find healthy ways to release emotions. It is important to regularly incorporate exercise in your routine to help balance your emotions and prevent health issues.

Jupiter in the Eighth House

Born with intuitive gifts and psychic abilities, you can help motivate others to find their purpose in life. You're extremely generous, loving, and kind and always give to those who need help. You have a naturally positive outlook.

Jupiter blesses you with good luck in your partnerships. You will benefit from other people's sacrifices. You are a person who is blessed with luck and often inherits money, land, and possessions. Be grateful and appreciate material assistance from others. It is important to commit to intimate relationships. Because you dislike selfish behaviors, you cut people off who are toxic or unhealthy. This placement helps protect against the more negative experiences and energies of the eighth house. There is often a guardian angel and protective energy that influences your life.

Saturn in the Eighth House

You are a person who restricts desires and has fears about intimate relationships. There is sometimes a karmic wound involving sexuality, trust, or loss of a loved one. With this placement, learning self-control and how to balance your emotional needs is a lesson. Sexual tensions are common, and repressing your urges causes a fear of intimacy. You feel pressured to find love and have intimate relationships. Work on healing your karmic issues by trusting others and being emotionally vulnerable.

Saturn likes to control things, so be cautious about having high expectations that can cause disappointment. It is important to balance stress and feelings of depression, perceived burdens, and your responsibilities. Focus on curbing negative thoughts and foster a more positive outlook.

Inheritances are often delayed with this placement, or there are problems with wills, real estate, or legal issues. Financial problems can occur with your partner or family.

Uranus in the Eighth House

You are a person who has psychic visions and flashes of the future. Unexpected changes in finances, relationships, intimacy, and death are associated with this placement. Uranus here brings unexpected financial and emotional benefits such as inheritances. It is also important to be prepared for sudden and unexpected losses such as divorce or financial issues. Be cautious about doing anything risky; drive safely and make sure to pay attention to surroundings.

You need freedom and dislike feeling trapped by obligations. It is important to heal your restless urges by learning to stay put and committing to things and people. Expressing your own individuality and eccentric nature in intimate relationships is very important.

Neptune in the Eighth House

Mystical experiences are common with this placement. Unexpected flashes, feelings, and thoughts give you insights into the future. Learn to trust your spiritual experiences and intuition. You have an increased sensitivity to energies and absorb everything going on in the environment. Develop strong boundaries to protect your energy field. It's important to spend time alone, contemplate feelings, and work on reducing stress.

This placement increases naivety. You have a very giving, trusting, and compassionate nature. Be cautious about other people's motives and don't let people take advantage of your kindness. Stop making excuses for people's bad behavior. Helping others brings contentment, but don't sacrifice yourself by taking on other people's problems. Be cautious about drinking alcohol or doing drugs due to physical sensitivities, and also be careful with medications.

You are a person who seeks a spiritual union with a partner. This placement craves romance and seeks a soul mate. Work on seeing situations, people, and yourself clearly. Trust your inner voice and intuition because it's usually right. Heal suffering by merging with a higher power and overcome addictive behaviors.

Pluto in the Eighth House

You are a person who is deep, secretive, and intuitive. You were born with a powerful ability to attract and heal others. Strong and controlling, you dislike fakeness and superficiality.

Sometimes others are intimidated by your intense presence and sense you can read their thoughts.

You will experience death, rebirth, and regenerative experiences. You are a wounded healer, and healing others helps heal your own pain. You are drawn to healing professions such as psychology and counseling where listening to people's problems and secrets is a daily practice.

Intimate relationships bring challenges, and you are learning to let go of your need for power and control. Taking things seriously, expecting commitment, and avoiding lighthearted conversations in relationships is common with Pluto in the eighth house. It is important to heal issues in your relationships by expressing your true feelings and emotions. Acknowledge your strong need for sexual bonding. Experience deep connections with others.

CHAPTER

SAGITTARIUS & THE NINTH HOUSE

Nickname: Sagittarius the Traveler

Symbol: The archer

Sun Sign Dates: November 22–December 21

Ruler: Jupiter

Rules: The ninth house; the hips, liver, and thighs

Sign Type: Fire, mutable

Polar Opposite Sign: Gemini

Tips for Healing: Seek freedom, travel, learn, practice faith

Sagittarius is a mutable sign, which means Sagittarians are known to be easygoing, adaptable, and adventurous. Sagittarians love freedom and are avid travelers. They are known to change direction at the last minute and adapt to their environment easily. As a fire sign, Sagittarians are independent, restless, straightforward, and eager to learn new things. They are optimistic and always try to see the positive side of a situation.

CHALLENGING ATTRIBUTES OF A SAGITTARIUS

Sagittarians are not the type of people who should sit at a desk all day. If the environment is uncomfortable or confining, it can cause restlessness and irritability. Sagittarians do their best work when they are free to come and go and are given full autonomy in their work environment.

POSITIVE ATTRIBUTES OF A SAGITTARIUS

Sagittarians enjoy being outdoors in nature and dislike being cooped up inside for too long. Feeling free to make decisions and discussing opinions in a straightforward way helps them feel better. They have a deep need to travel and study many different topics because they are always seeking knowledge. A career that requires travel is very satisfying for them. Driving in a car all day can be soothing; making short trips throughout the day from place to place and being allowed to travel for personal pleasure bring happiness.

The planet Jupiter rules this sign and blesses Sagittarians with good luck, generosity, and positivity. Sagittarians are happy, jovial, and positive even when stressed, and they stay in a good mood most of the time. When things are challenging, they dig deep and find that spirit of hope within to bounce back. They focus on the good things in life and genuinely want the best for others. They are optimistic and enjoy socializing with many different kinds of people. Extremely generous, they enjoy doing things for those they care about and are known as a supportive friend. Sagittarians are fun to be around and bring out the best in people. They are known to give honest, direct feedback in a kind way. Other people always know where they stand with a Sagittarius and appreciate their honesty.

The ninth house is associated with travel, religion, and higher education. The ninth house is ruled by Sagittarius, making Sagittarians naturally spiritual, intelligent, philosophical, and open-minded. Many Sagittarians are born with a faith in a higher power. Nurturing intuition and seeking answers within becomes a part of daily life. Sagittarians are searching for something bigger than themselves, so seeking a connection with religion brings comfort. Sometimes they are attracted to religious positions where they can help others find hope, courage, and strength. They may also seek a more alternative spiritual path and study meditation, energy healing, or New Age topics.

Reading, writing, and learning brings growth and purpose. Even if they do not attend college, Sagittarians are always learning things and studying various subjects on their own. They are extremely intelligent and have an excellent memory. Careers in research, teaching, and higher education are rewarding and bring Sagittarians happiness. Because they collect experiences through their travels and studies, they experience joy when sharing their knowledge and ideas with others.

Relationships with a Sagittarius

Sagittarians have a strong independent streak and might have difficulties with relationships. This often occurs because they have difficulties with commitment. Even when they truly care about someone, they keep a part of themselves separate and never fully allow themselves to settle down. When things become too comfortable or routine, Sagittarians grow bored because they need adventure and growth in relationships. If they feel controlled, possessed, or shamed about their independent nature, they may run for the hills and end relationships abruptly. Many choose to remain unmarried and value time alone.

Sagittarians are seeking something in the distance and reaching toward the unknown. They need the freedom to explore the many things that help them grow into a mature person. Finding individuals that support their quest is important and might help them maintain long-term relationships. If not, Sagittarians are perfectly content being single and traveling the world alone or with friends.

When Sagittarians are in a relationship, it is crucial for their partner to trust them and allow them to do their own thing. When they come back from running around all day doing what they wanted to do, then they will feel cheerful, happy, and ready to spend quality time with their loved ones.

Sagittarius Tips for Transformation

Highly intelligent, Sagittarians are born with a desire for change and exploration. It is common for them to try to shake things up when life becomes stable, boring, or routine.

Make Commitments

Sagittarians transform when they allow themselves to fully commit to other people. Sagittarians need to feel free. Being able to roam with nothing holding them back from pursuing their dreams is important to them. Because they don't like being pinned down, Sagittarians have a hard time figuring out what they want in intimate relationships. When things get too serious, they may break things off quickly. They need to learn that they can have both: a relationship and the freedom to experience adventure.

Balance Restlessness

Sagittarians crave movement and enjoy being outdoors in nature. These activities are good for their body, mind, and soul. But transformation occurs when Sagittarians balance their constant need for movement with time for relaxation. They need to make time to ground themselves and slow down. Learning to listen to their body and taking time to nurture it will help balance health.

Seek Knowledge

Sagittarians are always seeking new information because they thrive in a learning environment. It is important for them to pursue hobbies that inspire new and creative ideas. They should avoid taking on too many responsibilities, however, because this could make them feel burdened and overwhelmed. Whatever Sagittarians decide to pursue, success comes naturally because they have high hopes and a positive attitude. When they are able to face the horizon and move forward freely and without inhibition, they learn to balance their expansive energy. They transform when they follow their own distinct path. A Sagittarius's adventurous spirit needs a constant change of scenery, and travel enables them to find that.

SAGITTARIUS TIPS FOR HEALING

Healing comes easier for Sagittarius than any other sign due to their positive nature. Sagittarians understand that negative thoughts can affect their health, so they are always trying to see the positive lesson in a difficult experience. Spending time outdoors, getting fresh air, and being in nature can be soothing and help reduce stress. Allowing themselves to depend on others and realizing they don't have to do everything on their own will help them overcome adversity. Relying on friends and family who are encouraging and supportive of their dreams can help them with challenges. They enjoy spending time socializing with people they care about.

Embrace Freedom

It is important for a Sagittarius's loved ones to trust their ability to make decisions without monitoring them; feeling free is important for their well-being and happiness. Having the ability to roam and move freely is soothing to their soul and critical to their overall health. Sagittarians also heal by spending time doing activities that involve physical or mental movement.

Travel

Traveling and exploring different cities, countries, and historic sites creates a greater appreciation for history. It is beneficial for Sagittarians to plan one special trip each year so they have something to look forward to. This will give them time to save money, plan trip details and excursions, and prepare for many special adventures.

Strengthen Your Faith

Out of all the signs, Sagittarians are the most blessed with inborn, natural faith that helps them overcome many devastating issues in life. Believing in a higher power gives Sagittarians the courage and purpose to overcome heartache. When bad things happen in their life, turning to God and having faith helps encourage healing. They believe that everything happens for a reason and purpose. Strength comes from faith even if Sagittarians don't follow a traditional religion. They always try to see the blessings in a situation and have a positive outlook, which is why they tend to heal more quickly than other signs.

Reduce Worry

A Sagittarius's vulnerable areas are the hips, liver, and thighs. Sciatic nerve issues and muscle spasms in the thighs and hamstrings are common. When they get older, their hips are prone to arthritis. Sagittarians should be cautious with their diet and limit their alcohol intake because the liver might be weakened by fatty foods and substances. Excessive worry can cause tension and anxiety. Finding time to explore by taking walks, hiking, and being outdoors in the fresh air is beneficial to their health.

SAGITTARIUS RESILIENCY

Sagittarians are positive people who seek faith. They bounce back from adversity by moving forward and looking toward the future. They never get stuck in the past for too long because they are always looking forward to their next adventure. Their desire for newness assists them during times of crisis and change. As a person who always tries to see the silver lining in bad situations, positive energy helps them overcome many obstacles. Something inside pushes them forward and helps keep that flicker of hope alive even in the middle of a terrible experience.

Sagittarians do not give up easily, and it takes a lot to keep them down. Luckily, they snap out of depression and sadness quickly by focusing on the blessings they have. Being hopeful helps maintain their faith in themselves and they prevail because they refuse to fall prey to negativity. Having a positive outlook encourages strength and resilience for themselves and others.

Sagittarians believe in the power of good thoughts and these thoughts attract blessings to their life. They believe in the law of attraction and in the power of manifestation. Trusting in a higher power can protect them and inspire them to become more resilient by helping them find strength and purpose when life gets tough.

Sagittarians benefit from having a spiritual routine, whether that is attending traditional church services, walking in nature, practicing yoga, or attending a meditation group once a week. Surrounding themselves with like-minded people helps them build resilience. Spending time with friends and having fun socializing helps them grow stronger as a person. Sagittarians have a gift for speaking the truth in a direct way and sharing their feelings and ideas with those closest to them helps Sagittarians overcome stress and confusion.

How to Support a Sagittarius

If there is a Sagittarius in your life, let them be free do whatever they want. Respect their need for freedom and adventure. Don't try to change them; accept who they are. Allow them to believe whatever they want to believe. Be spontaneous and positive around them. Explore the world with them and go on adventures together.

SAGITTARIUS REFLECTION QUESTIONS

- How do you make time for travel, and where do you want to go?
- How do you find ways to feel spontaneous and adventurous?
- Is there anything you need to heal?
- What personality traits help you become more resilient?
- How do you handle stress and anxiety?

SAGITTARIUS AFFIRMATIONS

- "I am thankful every day for the blessings in my life. I am grateful that I am alive and healthy."
- "I have faith. I believe that everything happens for a reason. I look for the silver lining in every cloud."
- "I am adventurous. I make time to explore because it brings me joy."
- "I love my body. I move my body to clear my mind. I am full of energy."

SAGITTARIUS SELF-CARE IDEAS

- Travel somewhere you have always wanted to explore.
- Take a college class or study a new subject that inspires you.
- Get outdoors and go hiking in nature.
- Create three positive affirmations to recite daily.

- List three self-care techniques you find helpful and make time to do those things.

- Draw a flower with seven petals. Write down one new self-care activity you want to implement in each of the petals. Then hang the flower on the wall as a reminder. Try to do one new self-care activity every day until you've incorporated them into your routine.

THE NINTH HOUSE

Being born with faith and a strong belief in something greater than ourselves is a true blessing. We have the ninth house to thank for this type of gift. The ninth house rules all issues related to religion, philosophy, belief, law, history, and higher education. Not only does the ninth house have to do with our desire to learn and study subjects, it's also the house of travel. Traveling to foreign countries and visiting exotic places are key for this house since it is known to rule faraway places and travel away from the homeland. It is not a surprise that Sagittarius, the wanderer, traveler, philosopher, and optimist, rules this house.

The energy of this house is positive and energizes and expands our awareness. When planets are placed in the ninth house, there is a desire to achieve honors in education and obtain degrees in subjects that are important to us. The energy of this house encourages diversity and creates an interest in different cultures. For example, someone with the sun placed in the ninth house might find themselves joining the military because living a military life introduces them to people from different backgrounds and allows them to live in a different country.

SAGITTARIUS & THE NINTH HOUSE   ☼   189

If you do not have planets in the ninth house, this is not a negative thing. It simply means that area of your life will not be as active. You will need to look at what sign is on the cusp of the ninth house to be able to see how that energy impacts higher education, travel, and religion. For instance, if you have Aquarius on the ninth house cusp, you might rebel against traditional religion and venture out on your own to find a spiritual path. You will be drawn to friends from different religions, cultures, and ethnicities. Knowledge and study will come easily for you, and you might want to study subjects that are revolutionary, futuristic, or technological.

If You Have Planets in the Ninth House

The ninth house encourages movement and expansion. You are freedom-loving and independent. You are always seeking to expand your knowledge by traveling, exploring, and learning more about the world. With planets placed here, there is a restlessness that can affect your life in many ways. It could manifest as a great desire to travel to Europe, a craving for foreign cuisine a few times a week, or falling in love with someone that was raised in another country. Moving around from place to place is common with ninth-house planets. It is important to recognize and embrace a fascination with anything that is foreign or different. Because you are adventurous and driven, you might find enjoyment in taking foreign language classes to broaden your vocabulary in preparation for future travel.

No matter how hard life may become or how your beliefs are tested, there is always a sense of understanding and faith that resonates from the ninth house. Even in the midst of disaster or the depths of depression, you will pick yourself up and hope for a better future. Your positive energy and uplifting attitude come naturally. The gifts of the ninth house are belief, faith, and optimism in the face of adversity. Learning to embrace your unique beliefs and experiences is something that takes great courage, and the ninth house can help you do that.

You have a strong faith and dogmatic belief system. Planets here can bring strong convictions and high standards when it comes to morality and justice. You might find it hard to sway from your childhood religious upbringing, or you might rebel against religion and embrace unorthodox belief systems. Struggling to find a spiritual path that brings comfort is common when planets are placed in the ninth house. Your faith may be tested at some point in your life, making you doubt things. This forces you to re-examine your beliefs about God.

The energy of the ninth house enhances strong opinions and convictions; you share your beliefs with others with great zeal. You easily convince others to care about your personal passions. Surrounding yourself with intellectual people who understand you is important and helps encourage friendly debate of topics such as history, politics, law, religion, and philosophy. Ninth-house people are natural teachers, and you can inspire others to learn new things because of your great enthusiasm.

You are often interested in ideas that differ from how you were raised. You shine when pursuing knowledge on your own. As a forever student, taking night classes, attending college, or pursuing self-study will help you fulfill your dreams. You have a strong desire to pursue higher learning and educational advancement, so it is important in finding a career that inspires growth and inspiration.

When planets are in the ninth house, there is a need for an environment that allows room to explore and is not restrictive. A home that is open and spacious helps you thrive, and when you own property, land, or animals, you feel free to do what you want. You are always seeking something but never quite understanding what that is. The energy of Jupiter pushes you forward and toward new horizons.

PLANETS IN THE NINTH HOUSE

If you have one or more planets in the ninth house, read the corresponding sections for tips for transformation, healing, and resilience.

Sun in the Ninth House

You are a person who is passionate about traveling and seeking answers. Voicing your opinions and making a difference in the world brings you fulfillment. Having conversations with people from all walks of life is one of your many talents. This placement makes you an excellent teacher because you have an enthusiasm for knowledge and sharing ideas. Many with this placement live in a foreign country at some time in their lives; some join the military.

Allow yourself to transform through exploration, adventure, and pursuing your dreams. It is important to study subjects that bring you happiness and challenge your views and beliefs. An inborn faith and optimistic outlook assist you in overcoming many obstacles.

Moon in the Ninth House

You are a person who feels comfort when experiencing new places and learning new things. Finding peace through travel is common with the moon placed here. But emotionally, you need change because you get bored with the same routines. Adventure fulfills your restless emotional nature. Sometimes you worry about not being able to travel because it's expensive, but you can find adventure anywhere you go, even if you just drive to the next town over. Allowing movement and exploration in your daily life helps balance your thoughts and emotions.

With the moon here, you learn lot about the world through conversation and by listening to stories other people tell. The more eccentric, unique, and different people are, the more intriguing you find them. You find emotional fulfillment from having a spiritual belief system or religious practice.

Mercury in the Ninth House

You are a person who is opinionated and intelligent. Spreading information and knowledge through all forms of communication brings comfort. Focused on the facts, you are able to detach from your emotions easily. Mercury placed here enhances natural writing talents and teaching skills. Sharing your thoughts, beliefs, and ideas through teaching brings success.

Mercury in the ninth house creates a positive, optimistic way of thinking that helps ward off unpleasant emotions such as depression, sadness, and anxiety. Changing and questioning your beliefs about traditional religion is likely to occur as you grow older.

Venus in the Ninth House

You are a person who accepts other cultures and ideas. When Venus is in the ninth house, there is an appreciation of foreign art, beauty, religion, and philosophy. You love to travel and have a desire to explore faraway places, so may choose to live in a foreign country. Your partners are often found while traveling and come from a different culture, ethnicity, or religious background. You may fall in love with someone from another country, or you may choose to marry someone who was raised very differently than you were. With this placement, it is important to develop relationships that allow freedom and adventure. Happiness comes from pursuing things you love and appreciate.

Mars in the Ninth House

You are a person who has a strong drive to express your religious and spiritual ideas. Joining the military is common with this placement because it allows travel to foreign countries and areas. Mars in the ninth house needs an outlet for its powerful energy. This placement creates an inborn faith that nothing can alter. You are known to fight for your beliefs and are passionate about pursuing your goals; nothing can stop you once you make up your mind. Fighting for your beliefs can sometimes cause others to see you as a religious zealot. Be careful not to force your beliefs on others and listen to other people's opinions, even if they are different from your own. Channel your passion into educational pursuits and ambitions. As a natural teacher, you will succeed in industries like publishing, teaching, and writing.

Jupiter in the Ninth House

You spend a lot of time studying things that bring you enjoyment. You are confident, generous, and hungry for knowledge. Your need for constant adventure can create restlessness. Traveling to foreign countries and meeting different people is fun and exciting. Embrace your need for freedom and independence. Stepping out of your comfort zone and exploring new things brings you good luck. Growth comes from travel and exploration.

Having a strong faith in a higher power is important for you. With this placement, you may be attracted to careers that enable you to share your opinions and views, such as education, publishing, ministry, or teaching. You are a person who has a positive way of expressing your views.

Saturn in the Ninth House

You are a person who can be rigid and dogmatic about your beliefs. One of your parents could have been very strict, forcing you to behave a certain way, which could have caused some resentment. Many with this placement live by a very rigid moral code that is deeply ingrained. If you learn to open up your mind about other religions and beliefs, it will bring greater self-awareness.

Sometimes you feel that you must work harder than others to attain your goals. It is important to address any burdens that prevent you from seeking higher education, such as financial concerns, fears, and debts. With Saturn placed here, overcoming fears about traveling far distances and taking more risks will help you grow as a person. If you work on communicating your ideas and expressing yourself, you will find greater balance in life.

Uranus in the Ninth House

If you had a traditional belief system growing up, it is tested by your desire to express a unique, eccentric belief system that goes against society's standards. You are a person who needs to explore new ideas. You may change your beliefs often. With this placement, you are known to rebel against traditional religion and anything that is restricted or narrow-minded.

Freedom is a necessity because you like having the flexibility to study interesting topics. You are always on an intellectual search for answers, and this placement means you are talented when it comes to research and higher education. Traveling to international destinations and exploring unique adventures brings you happiness. Joining the Peace Corps, traveling to a remote jungle, or backpacking across Europe are right up your alley.

Neptune in the Ninth House

You are a person who possesses an extraordinary faith in a higher power. Spiritual beliefs and studies are important for your growth. Your blind faith can be supportive when difficult situations arise, but it can also create an avoidance of practical responsibilities. This placement indicates a need to heal spiritual doubts or the suffering that can come from traditional religion. Traveling to spiritual sites is impactful. Be cautious about getting lured into a religious cult or abused by people who take advantage of your trusting nature. It is helpful for you to develop stronger boundaries and to be more practical about your beliefs.

This placement indicates that there could be difficulties or setbacks when it comes to pursuing higher education. You may have a lack of trust in your own abilities. Believe in yourself and trust your ability to achieve your educational goals.

Pluto in the Ninth House

You are a person who is passionate about your beliefs. You were born with a compulsive need to share ideas about faith with others. You have strong opinions, and you are a formidable advocate because you are deeply attached to what you believe in. You are also a transformative teacher. You have a gift for research and can dig deep to find answers to life's problems.

Pluto in the ninth house is on an intense journey to find meaning in the world. At some point in your life, your belief system was completely transformed. Growth, transformation, and experiencing intense emotions regarding religion, philosophy, and education are common with this placement. Because you have a thirst for anything spiritual and religious, transformation and growth come through travel, movement, and adventure.

CHAPTER

CAPRICORN & THE TENTH HOUSE

Nickname: Capricorn the Achiever

Symbol: The goat

Sun Sign Dates: December 22–January 19

Ruler: Saturn

Rules: The tenth house; the knees, joints, and skin

Sign Type: Earth, cardinal

Polar Opposite Sign: Cancer

Tips for Healing: Relax, release control, find work-life balance

C apricorn is a cardinal earth sign. Capricorns are known to be ambitious, successful, driven, organized, practical, determined, and achievement oriented. One of the hardest-working signs in the zodiac, Capricorns are known for pushing hard to achieve goals. Born with a strong work ethic, Capricorns often neglect other responsibilities for career progression. Just like the goat who climbs up the side of a mountain, it might take them more time than others, but eventually they will reach the top. Capricorns are always pushing themselves to achieve greater heights, and their strength and determination bring opportunities for leadership positions.

CHALLENGING ATTRIBUTES OF A CAPRICORN

Being ruled by the planet Saturn makes Capricorns feel restricted; they have a sense of obligation to take care of those they love. Naturally quiet and introverted, in social situations they are not comfortable expressing their emotions. Capricorns tend to repress their thoughts and emotions. They do not like feeling vulnerable and will work hard to appear to be in control of everything at all times.

Sometimes Capricorns become so focused on work goals that they lose sight of their own inner emotions and needs. They are also known to neglect family responsibilities and their home life when they are experiencing work stress.

POSITIVE ATTRIBUTES OF A CAPRICORN

The tenth house is ruled by Capricorn. As the father figure of the zodiac, Capricorns are blessed with wisdom, practical advice, and a sense of loyalty. They are known to be serious and responsible people. Even from a young age, they feel more mature than others. Known to look and act older, they prefer to spend time with adults they can look up to. Yes, Capricorns are serious people, but they actually have a witty, sarcastic sense of humor and are talented at making people laugh in unexpected moments.

Capricorns want to appear stoic and in control at all times because they believe this will win the respect of others. A successful career where they have a position of power and supervise others is a main priority. Capricorns are natural leaders and have a good business sense. Careers in the public eye are a good choice for Capricorns. They also have a gift for managing finances and money.

RELATIONSHIPS WITH A CAPRICORN

Capricorns are not comfortable with public displays of affection. They experience difficulties in relationships because other people perceive them as cold and calculating. The truth is, they are caring people, but rigidity and shyness sometimes get in the way. Capricorns are known to be hard on themselves and sometimes deny their emotions. Capricorns are shy, private, and insecure about expressing their feelings unless they trust the other person. It takes time for a Capricorn to fully believe that someone else is worthy of their trust.

Capricorns are realists with natural street smarts that help them understand how to survive in the practical world. They are extremely responsible, loyal, and practical, and everyone in their life knows they are someone who can be relied on. It is important for Capricorns to find friends who can help them achieve success and support their goals. Naturally cautious, controlling their pessimistic nature and learning to think more positively will improve their life.

Capricorn Tips for Transformation

Capricorns are known to be old souls who are wise beyond their years, but being super responsible all the time can be exhausting. It is important for Capricorns to balance their own needs by taking time to unwind and recover their energy. Thinking positive thoughts helps Capricorns transform, removes pessimistic tendencies, and relaxes their cautious nature.

Celebrate Your Achievements

Capricorns transform by climbing the ladder of success. Through hard work and determination, they slowly achieve each goal they set for themselves. Sometimes it takes them longer to obtain success or career progression because they have to learn to utilize patience. Capricorns desire recognition, but they need to value themselves and their own achievements instead of searching for others' acknowledgment.

Enjoy the Present

Capricorns find motivation and passion by working toward things they want. They rarely give up on their goals. Even after experiencing struggles in life, Capricorns move up the ladder of success by having a positive attitude. Transforming the old version of themselves into a more powerful person happens when they are focused on being in the present moment.

Challenge Rigid Tendencies

With time, Capricorns can change their rigid thoughts and negative beliefs. Sometimes they restrict themselves so much that they never stop to enjoy life. Transformation occurs when they allow time for fun and stop being so hard on themselves.

Capricorns must overcome their rigidity, express their feelings, embrace spontaneity, and enjoy life. Embracing their sensitive side, minimizing controlling behaviors, and learning to communicate better will help them balance many areas of life. Capricorns are known to hide their emotions because they are afraid of appearing weak or being hurt, but they need to learn how to nurture their emotions instead of repressing them.

Capricorn Tips for Healing

Capricorns are great at taking care of their physical needs, but they need to make an effort to take care of their emotional needs too.

Balance Work and Family

Capricorns heal feelings of loneliness and stress when they get away from their desk. They need time to unplug from all work activities, deadlines, and responsibilities. Eventually Capricorns realize that work and financial success do not always bring love and happiness. Capricorns heal when they take a break from working to spend time with family.

In relationships, Capricorns tend to focus solely on providing security for their loved ones, but they heal relationships when they understand that their loved ones want to connect with them emotionally and spend quality time together too. Capricorns might have regrets later in life if they miss out on having fun or don't make time to relax with family and friends. The older they get, the more they realize the importance of enjoying life because time flies by. Capricorns need to realize that work will always be there, but children grow up and friends will move on without them if they don't put effort into strengthening their relationships. Creating a healthy work-life balance is key for Capricorns to find happiness.

Release Control

Helping others in practical ways and always feeling like they have to be the one to fix things are Capricorn traits. But being in total control of the outcome of situations sometimes backfires. Other people do not like to be told what to do, and Capricorns have to release the need to control the behaviors of others because it pushes people away.

Healing comes when Capricorns can accept the fact that they can't control those they care about. Telling people what they should do and having high expectations of others can cause relationship issues. Learning to let go and flowing with the natural energy of life will be beneficial.

Take Breaks

Capricorns will find greater healing when they work on releasing their inhibitions and learn to express themselves in a variety of ways. Overcoming and addressing depressive thoughts, dark moods, and irritability will help them heal. They need to allow time for fun and leisure. Capricorns need to learn that they don't always have to be climbing the mountain. Taking breaks will help them recover and rejuvenate their passion and energy.

Make Time to Relax

Capricorns' vulnerable areas are the knees, skin, and joints. The knees are prone to injuries and sprains, so it's important to stretch fully before physical activity. Excessive stress can cause skin problems like shingles, eczema, and acne. Arthritis is a common complaint, so they would benefit from using a sauna. Maintain a good work-life balance and make time for relaxation. Making time to get fresh air and pursuing fun hobbies helps reduce stress.

CAPRICORN RESILIENCY

Capricorns are achievement seekers. Their resilience comes from targeting goals and putting all their energy into achieving them. Practical and calculated, they do not like to rush toward their milestones, and they rarely get distracted from what they want. Capricorns have an uncanny ability to know exactly when they need to take action. Good luck comes from listening to their gut instincts and trusting intuitive feelings. They are known to overcome any obstacle that gets in their way with sheer determination. Patience is a virtue, and they know what it takes to strategically work toward success by overcoming many unpleasant situations.

Time helps Capricorn become wiser and more prepared for challenges. If they don't get what they want right away or life blocks them from reaching their goals, they never stop trying. Capricorns will rethink and re-strategize plans to adjust to the roadblocks that life throws their way because they are achievers, believers, and doers. They bounce back from adversity and know the difference between their needs and their wants. They typically put their needs first and sacrifice things that are not lasting or that will not benefit them in the future. Being naturally responsible and mature helps Capricorn adapt to hard times and challenges.

How to Support a Capricorn

If there is a Capricorn in your life, encourage them to communicate how they feel and connect with their emotions. Let them know they can trust you so they will be more vulnerable. Work hard and show them you are practical and responsible. Be a present and stable influence in their life. Help them learn to relax and have more fun. Tell jokes and make them smile and laugh. Love and accept them for who they are. Let them make plans and take the lead.

Capricorn Reflection Questions

- How do you achieve your goals and career ambitions?
- How do you balance work and family?
- Is there anything you need to heal?
- What personality traits help you become more resilient?
- How do you handle stress and anxiety?

Capricorn Affirmations

- "I am resilient. I overcome any obstacles in my path."
- "I find the light in the darkest of situations."
- "I make time for my hobbies. Relaxing is just as important as working hard."
- "Even when I feel like I am climbing a mountain, it is okay to take breaks now and then."

Capricorn Self-Care Ideas

- Go on vacation. Get away from work and take time to relax.

- Do not take work home with you. Don't check your work email when you're at home.

- Go out to eat at a fancy restaurant with someone special.

- Create three positive affirmations to recite daily.

- List three self-care techniques you find helpful and make time to do those things.

- Draw a flower with seven petals. Write down one new self-care activity you want to implement in each of the petals. Then hang the flower on the wall as a reminder. Try to do one new self-care activity every day until you've incorporated them into your routine.

THE TENTH HOUSE

Most of us have to work hard to make money to support ourselves financially. Sometimes we may get lucky and end up working in a career field we enjoy, but often we just take the best job we can get to pay our bills. The tenth house shows what type of career we are drawn to and interested in. The energy of this house can also shed light on where we find success and prestige. This is the house of hard work, ambition, public image, career advancement, and politics.

The energy of this house causes some people to work hard to reach the top, while others might decide to manipulate or use others to gain their career success. As the achiever of the zodiac, Capricorn rules the tenth house. The energy of this house forces us to push ourselves and climb up the mountain, just like the goat. Putting in the work is a lesson of the tenth house. People with tenth-house planets often start at a low-level job making minimum wage and get promoted because they push themselves; they want to reach their career goals and aren't afraid of getting their hands dirty and putting in the work. The rise to the top can be effortless if there are positive planets in the tenth house, but the view from the top can be lonely.

Tenth-house energy can manifest by helping us make money and finding practical solutions to problems.

If you don't have planets in the tenth house, this is not a bad thing. This just means that you will not have major life lessons related to career, the public, and work. You will need to look at the sign on the cusp of the tenth house to see what energy impacts your career and achievements. For instance, if you have Gemini on the tenth house cusp, you will need a career that allows short journeys, movement, and freedom. Being tied to a desk will be difficult, and you need to get outside or take breaks. You grow bored with mundane tasks and would benefit by having two jobs, or from having a hobby on the side that you could do to make extra income.

If You Have Planets in the Tenth House

The tenth house's goal is to help us understand what we are good at and what type of work we need to do. The sign that falls on the tenth house cusp often shows us which career field will benefit us. The tenth house cusp is also called the midheaven.

Planet placements in the tenth house bring a practical approach, a sense of purpose, and a successful public life. Seeking stability and having a stable career is a big part of your overall well-being.

If you have planets in the tenth house, you would benefit from a job in public service, politics, real estate, business, government, finance, or law. You may also be drawn to the military. You admire rank and try to emulate the characteristics of those who are in power. You are focused on obtaining a high-status position as a supervisor or authority figure.

You are an excellent addition to any work environment because you bring a strong work ethic and high stamina. Intrinsically motivated, you work hard on accomplishing tasks, planning for the future, and organizing the office. You are incredibly responsible, and your coworkers come to you for advice. It is second nature for you to step in and tell people what needs to be done and how to do it efficiently. You are an excellent planner and have great patience. If you are not in a supervisory position, you need to experience full autonomy at work so you can do your job unimpeded. You would enjoy owning your own business and making your own rules. There is no doubt that you will achieve anything you set your mind to.

You have a strong desire to be financially independent and accumulate status, power, and money. You want others to see you as successful. Planets in the tenth house affect self-esteem, and it is important for you to feel appreciated and valued for the work you do. There is no greater feeling than working in a job you love while having the respect of your supervisor, coworkers, and colleagues. You have a need to be recognized and honored for the hard work you do and love receiving awards and promotions. But just because you have a successful career does not mean the rest of your life will be happy; remember the importance of balancing all areas of life.

Ambitious and driven to achieve career goals, from a young age you thought about the career you would have someday. In your early years you enjoyed participating in clubs, sports, and activities like student government. You work hard for everything you have and do not expect the world to give you anything. With planets in the tenth house, you have high expectations of others, and it is important to realize that not everyone has the same work standards as you.

In your mind, others have wisdom and experience that you can learn from. It is second nature to respect those who have gone before you, and you often take advantage of apprenticeship opportunities. You will benefit from elders taking you under their wing. Developing connections with others and business partnerships can help promote career advancement.

Sometimes it is difficult for you to find time to relax and unwind. You spend a lot of time at the office focused on tasks, and you need to be careful about spending too much time at work. Be careful about neglecting your health, family, and friends due to being overly focused on achievements. Taking care of your family financially equates to success in your mind, but you need to be careful not to neglect the emotional needs of those closest to you.

When planets are placed in the tenth house, you are meant to learn lessons associated with your father figure. This relationship needs to be valued, nurtured, and healed.

Planets in the Tenth House

If you have one or more planets in the tenth house, read the corresponding section for tips for transformation, healing, and resilience.

Sun in the Tenth House

Being successful and making money is important to you. This placement creates a need to be in the limelight or publicly recognized. Positions of leadership and being in the public eye come naturally, but you may find that being behind the scenes helps create a greater balance.

You are a person who finds their identity by working hard and having a career. It is important that you feel appreciated, valued by your superiors, and respected for your strong work ethic. Changing your mind about what success looks like can help you find greater happiness and improve your self-esteem. Having a job where you are in charge is a goal, but don't forget to take time for relaxation and family responsibilities.

Moon in the Tenth House

You are a person who finds emotional comfort in having a successful career path. Working is important for your emotional stability, and the moon here creates a lot of worries about having a career. You are focused on finding the perfect job and worry about not being able to achieve the things you set out to do. Finding a secure job will bring stability, which is what you truly value. Avoid staying in a job just because of the financial security it brings. It is important to realize that doing something that makes you happy is the most important thing.

Feelings about the work you do can cause ups and downs. Try to adapt to the changes that come and trust your instincts. Exploring opportunities for greater responsibility at work might help you find the recognition you crave.

Mercury in the Tenth House

You are a person who spends a lot of time thinking about your career. Communicating what you want at work is one way to attain your dreams. With Mercury here, planning a career path in a logical, practical, detached way is common. Allow yourself to change your mind about what type of career you want. It is important not to act on impulses, but on practicality and intellect. Thinking things through and analyzing goals will help you prioritize what you really want.

Utilize your knowledge and skills to pursue careers where you can market your gifts. Focus on communicating and expressing your innovative ideas. Sharing your thoughts with trusted coworkers helps create feelings of support, but be cautious about gossiping and telling people private things because they could be exposed publicly.

Venus in the Tenth House

You are a person who cares about appearances and puts work before your relationships. Finding a peaceful, harmonious career where you can express your artistic abilities or creativity is important. Venus in the tenth house creates good luck with coworkers, bringing peace and support. You know people in leadership positions and can benefit from those relationships, as they can help you achieve your career goals.

You work hard and struggle to express your feelings. Finding a balance between work and romance can be challenging. With this placement, meeting people through work is common. You may start dating someone you met while traveling to a conference. Developing relationships with people who are older, wiser, mature, and more successful than you can bring happiness.

Mars in the Tenth House

You are a person who is very driven to succeed in your career. Remember that you don't need someone else's approval to feel successful. Ambitious at heart, you are always planning how to achieve everything you want. Born with great stamina, energy, and drive, you value working hard. You overcome all obstacles with sheer determination. Watch out for being too competitive with others in the workplace. You may experience conflict with coworkers or those in positions of authority because you feel that you must respect people in order to work for them.

Nurturing relationships at work, controlling your temper, and finding ways to collaborate will assist you in reaching your goals. It is important to balance your strong desires by recognizing that family, friends, and coworkers are an important part of your journey. This placement often indicates a strained relationship with your father figure, and it is important to heal this bond.

Jupiter in the Tenth House

You are a person who has a positive outlook. Optimistic, cheery, and open-minded, you attract many allies. You are blessed with a successful career, and you may benefit from being in the public eye. Jupiter in the tenth house indicates that you are generous to others, but taking care of yourself is just as important.

Acknowledge your need for adventure and independence in the work environment. Sitting at a desk could be difficult. Take time to stretch, walk, and enjoy fresh air. Feeling restless at work and experiencing boredom are common, so working two different jobs might bring happiness. Make time for travel because exploration and movement are important.

Saturn in the Tenth House

You are a disciplined worker with a controlling personality. Serious and responsible, others can depend on you to get the job done. This placement can lead to working long hours and striving for perfection. Leadership positions come naturally, but you can be perceived as strict and authoritarian. Feeling respected at work is critical for your happiness. Sometimes you feel you do not get the recognition you deserve or that career success is blocked in some way. Controlling pessimistic tendencies will help you feel better in the long run. Face your karmic learning related to attaining success, recognition, and achievement. Saturn placed here indicates a need to change your relationship toward success and to learn to find time to enjoy life. Patience is a virtue, and success comes when you wait for the right timing.

Uranus in the Tenth House

You are a person who experiences many changes and upheavals in your career. Accept change and transformation involving work responsibilities, tasks, and achievements. Struggles with finding stable employment are common. Feeling free is important, but so is following the rules. This placement creates a restless nature and can cause problems with authority figures. With Uranus in the tenth house, you feel a need to rebel from traditional career paths. Find a career that allows you to be creative, unique, and eccentric. Science, technology, and innovative careers would be good options.

Neptune in the Tenth House

Idealistic, naive, and innocent, fantasizing about the perfect job can create sadness when it is never found. Expressing your artistic and creative talents in a job will bring greater contentment.

Working in music, entertainment, or the performing arts can bring happiness. Face your illusions about success, as Neptune in the tenth house rewards you when you see things clearly and help others who are suffering, struggling, or in need. Confusion about your place in the world is common, and you might find it difficult to figure out which career path to take. Careers such as social work, addiction counseling, or psychology would also be a good fit.

Pluto in the Tenth House

You are a person who desires a successful career. This placement creates a need for power and a strong feeling of ambition. Transformation occurs naturally in your work environment because you push yourself and others to change. It is important to experience constant growth in your career field, so changing jobs often helps alleviate feelings of stagnation and boredom. It is more beneficial, though, to learn to stay firmly planted. Work through difficulties with coworkers and authority figures in the workplace. Work on your issues related to power and control, or your relationships could suffer. Being a leader comes naturally, but you need to balance your powerful emotions.

Charming others is one of your strengths. Pluto in the tenth house gives you a powerful presence when you are on stage or in the public arena. Accept transformative change and heal through your public image. Recognition will bring greater growth.

Aquarius & the Eleventh House

Nickname: Aquarius the Humanitarian

Symbol: The water bearer

Sun Sign Dates: January 20–February 18

Ruler: Uranus

Rules: The eleventh house; the ankles and circulatory system

Sign Type: Air, fixed

Polar Opposite Sign: Leo

Tips for Healing: Connect emotionally, nurture friendships, join groups

A quarius is an air sign notorious for being eccentric, intellectual, and detached from emotions. Their first reaction in any situation is to think rather than react, and many times their emotions never come into the picture. Aquarians are known to change direction when they find something more unique, intriguing, or challenging. The element of air makes them open-minded, but as a fixed sign, they are known to also be inflexible in some of their beliefs and opinions. They are slow to change something they have embraced as truth. Aquarians possess personality traits that are both practical and unstable. As lovers of freedom, being able to express their individuality and creativity is important.

Challenging Attributes of an Aquarius

Rebelling against authority figures and cultural rules that they feel do not make sense is second nature to an Aquarius. Nothing is more frustrating for an Aquarius than being perceived as normal or boring.

Many of their friends will recognize that Aquarians have difficulty expressing emotions. They are more intellectual about things, and it is not easy for them to process their emotions. Because of this, they are often perceived as cold and aloof. Some people are uncertain about approaching an Aquarius because they intuitively feel that Aquarians are not interested in getting to know them. The truth is that Aquarians would help anyone who needs it; they just don't like being swept up in huge displays of emotion.

Because they are ruled by the planet Uranus, Aquarians interact with others in an impersonal way. This is why Aquarians might be attracted to the medical field, perhaps as a surgeon or radiologist.

POSITIVE ATTRIBUTES OF AN AQUARIUS

Aquarians are the scientists, inventors, innovators, and original thinkers of the zodiac. Extremely intelligent with a photographic memory, pursuing knowledge and spending time studying comes easily to them. Research and investigation enable them to think outside the box to find new solutions to problems. Although they are naturally smart, Aquarians need to be challenged and supported by teachers and mentors to reach their true potential. They can be rebellious in a classroom environment if there is not enough room to explore.

Born with an innate desire to be seen as a unique and original individual, Aquarians want to stand out in a crowd. Living an eccentric lifestyle is important for self-expression. They might enjoy studying subjects that are taboo or have a desire to challenge other's belief systems. Aquarians may shock people by dressing strangely, pursuing unique hobbies, or showing up with a new piercing or tattoo. They feel alive when they can express their personality without restriction.

The eleventh house is ruled by Aquarius and relates to humanitarian work, friendship, groups, hopes, wishes, and dreams. Others find it easy to talk with Aquarius because they are attentive listeners who help ground others. Making many acquaintances and becoming friends with people from different walks of life brings an Aquarius happiness. Supporting people by being part of a humanitarian group is what they do best. Emotional distance enables them to help others; born with natural boundaries, they avoid taking on other people's emotions like some of the other signs do.

Being forced to conform to rules or others' expectations can cause difficulties. Aquarians are known to support equal rights causes and can be found at the head of a picket line or marching on Capitol Hill. They are not afraid to fight against something that stifles other people's freedom of expression. Intellectually, they are more than capable of winning opponents to their side. Because an Aquarius is well versed in many different subjects, they make excellent teachers and group leaders. When they have a common goal, dream, or mission with others, they shine. If they can be a part of a large group with a shared mission, they feel happy and fulfilled.

Aquarius can be very unorthodox, or they can be rigid in their beliefs. There is always a need to seek new ways to express their creativity, individuality, and knowledge. When they are able to fully express themselves and their intellectual gifts, Aquarians find fulfillment.

Uranus energy unleashes itself in an Aquarius's life, and it can be difficult for them to fully commit to people. Maintaining a sense of individuality and freedom in relationships is important, and for this reason, Aquarians often have many platonic friendships. It is important for Aquarians to have people in their life who can challenge them mentally because they are prone to restlessness and have a habit of moving on when they get bored. As long as they are able to express their personality and have a mental connection with someone, feelings can slowly develop.

When in a relationship, sometimes Aquarians find it difficult to be physically intimate with another person and prefer talking and sharing ideas. Aquarians need to find relationship partners that accept the strange, eccentric, and weird parts of their personality. A loner at heart, they enjoy being by themselves to focus on creative hobbies. If a friend or partner makes an Aquarius feel controlled or if they are too clingy, this will lead to relationship problems. Learning that they can still have autonomy in relationships and keep their independent spirit is one of their greatest challenges.

AQUARIUS TIPS FOR TRANSFORMATION

Aquarians transform when they are able to pursue their deepest desires, even if they are different than others'. When there are no obstacles in the way, they can move swiftly toward all the things they want to learn.

Continue Setting Boundaries

Aquarians have a tendency to detach from emotions because they see them as irrelevant; thinking about things is preferred because using logic to solve problems comes naturally. Emotional detachment helps Aquarians keep solid boundaries with loved ones. This ability helps protect their personal space and prevents them from taking on other people's problems. Because of this, Aquarians are able to help others in an objective way and are known to give good advice.

Express Your Uniqueness

Transformation comes when Aquarians are able to express their individuality and unique tastes. Aquarians might dye their hair purple and get a tattoo or piercing to see the reaction of their parents, friends, or society. They can go through phases of rebellion where they are searching for the right way to express their individuality and uniqueness. Aquarians need to learn to express their true identity and different beliefs without fear of being criticized. Being part of a group of people who believe and fight for similar causes brings them comfort. They grow stronger when they develop the confidence to challenge societal rules and traditions.

Seek Freedom

Transformation happens when Aquarians are allowed the autonomy to do things at their own pace. The more independent they feel, the more they trust themselves, which makes them more capable of achieving their dreams, ambitions, and goals. Expressing themselves without fear of judgment and feeling accepted by their friend group are important. Aquarians have a desire to break free from all outside restrictions, and they will challenge others to find their own unique expression.

Challenge Beliefs

Aquarians might rebel and follow a different spiritual path than the one they were taught growing up. They find true happiness when they accept the fact that there is nothing wrong with having different beliefs and questioning rules. The act of challenging outdated beliefs will help Aquarians find out who they truly are. (They should just be careful not to stir things up simply for attention, because then they may become known as a rebel who causes chaos.) Being able to follow their inspiration is the goal. When Aquarians have the ability to pursue goals, hopes, wishes, and dreams freely, they will transform. They need to remember to reach for the stars because they have the ability to get there.

AQUARIUS TIPS FOR HEALING

Because they are unemotional people, others may perceive Aquarians as cold and detached. Aquarians can sometimes find it hard to express their emotions or show weakness. Sometimes their family and friends feel Aquarius is not capable of understanding the feelings of others because of their detachment. Born a deep thinker, they like to give advice based solely on logic and intellect.

Express Your Emotions

Healing comes when Aquarians balance their thoughts and allow themselves to get comfortable with their feelings. Listening to their inner self when they experience loss or pain can help Aquarians overcome heartbreak, but thoughts will not always be the solution they need. When Aquarians are struggling with challenges, it's good for them to rely on friends who will listen and share wisdom. Healing happens when Aquarians allow others to help them solve their problems.

Connect to Others

Aquarians naturally intellectualize everything and try to find practical ways to deal with crises. They are typically comfortable with the unexpected and can adapt easily when change affects their life because Uranus blesses them with an adaptable energy to move forward after adversity. When Aquarians are struggling, though, surrounding themselves with acquaintances and participating in groups brings healing. It is not good for them to be alone or to isolate themselves; it is important that they practice connecting with others in a deeper way.

Aquarians are capable of overcoming obstacles when they develop coping skills and focus on pursuing their lofty goals. Helping others in some way makes them feel like they are making a difference in the world, and participating in groups encourages healing. Helping others on a grand scale is important, and making a huge impact is part of their mission. Aquarians prefer helping people in larger groups versus one-on-one relationships. Volunteering at a food shelter or working with neglected children satisfies their desire to serve.

Embrace Your Creativity

Aquarians heal by rebelling against restrictions and releasing all of the expectations that other people have for them. They feel lighter when they can follow their own unique path regardless of how others feel. Healing comes by pursuing their inner truth and developing independent beliefs. Aquarians should get comfortable with being different, standing out in a crowd, and being noticed for their specialness. Because Aquarians are creative thinkers, they have inspiring ideas that pop up unexpectedly. It is beneficial to keep a journal to jot down their creative ideas so they don't forget them. Healing comes through writing and teaching others what they know.

Prioritize Physical Activity

Aquarians' vulnerable areas are the ankles, shins, and circulatory system. The ankles are prone to sprains and injuries. Making time to exercise helps with hypertension and circulation. Excessive stress can cause nervous disorders, accidents, and allergies. Aquarians typically have good health and remain mentally active throughout life, but physical activity might be difficult to implement or maintain, causing excess weight gain.

Aquarius Resiliency

When life forces them to change unexpectedly, Aquarians embrace these changes and are able to flow with the new energy, unlike other signs. When challenges happen, Aquarians are known to focus on the future. They bounce back quickly from tough times. They use their logical mind and practical approach to move forward with an optimistic belief in the future. Aquarians usually have a positive attitude and friendly spirit that helps them overcome obstacles and roadblocks.

A free spirit, Aquarians enjoy anything that helps them grow as a unique individual. Aquarians become more resilient when they continue to learn about themselves and their personality. Strength comes when they don't allow the opinions of others to affect their lifestyle or choices. When they are allowed to make their own choices and are able to move freely, they are capable of doing great things. As a seeker of knowledge, sharing their perspective can help in the healing process.

Aquarians benefit from joining groups and communicating with others that share creative ideas. Sharing similar interests with others and pursuing their hobbies and dreams will give them something to look forward to. Spending time with friends can help distract them during difficult times.

How to Support an Aquarius

If there is an Aquarius in your life, become their best friend and stimulate their mind. Share your dreams and creative ideas with them. Allow them the freedom to be who they want to be. Don't be afraid to be weird and different—they respect that. Broaden your intellectual pursuits and find out what is important to them. Get used to unpredictability and accept that they need variety in their lives. Do not be judgmental; have an open mind.

AQUARIUS REFLECTION QUESTIONS

- How do you express your eccentric and original ideas?
- How do you handle your need for freedom?
- Is there anything you need to heal?
- What personality traits help you become more resilient?
- How do you handle stress and anxiety?

AQUARIUS AFFIRMATIONS

- "I find solutions for almost any problem. I am intelligent and courageous."
- "I love my friends. I have a strong support system full of people who want the best for me."
- "I am unique. My thoughts are my own. I am unapologetically me."

AQUARIUS SELF-CARE IDEAS

- Read self-help books, implement the law of attraction, and utilize a journal to verbalize your hopes, wishes, and dreams.
- Spend time sharing creative ideas in groups or with friends.
- Express your restless energy by challenging your mind.

- Create three positive affirmations to recite daily.

- List three self-care techniques you find helpful and make time to do those things.

- Draw a flower with seven petals. Write down one new self-care activity you want to implement in each of the petals. Then hang the flower on the wall as a reminder. Try to do one new self-care activity every day until you've incorporated them into your routine.

THE ELEVENTH HOUSE

Anytime more than two individuals get together for a common goal, we need to thank the eleventh house. The eleventh house is often associated with friendship and acquaintances, but most importantly, it rules group behavior and humanitarian work.

The energy of this house is intellectual, not emotional. Aquarius is the sign that rules the eleventh house, so there is a tendency to form relationships that are more platonic and based on friendship. Aquarians are known for their coolness, aloofness, and tendency to intellectualize, so the eleventh house has a very mental approach to serving others.

This is the house of organizations that seek to help large groups of people on a broader scale; this is the house of serving others through detached service. Those with planets in the eleventh house listen to people's problems, but they have an uncanny ability to not take on those problems. Eleventh-house people are all about helping others on a larger scale in a detached, logical, practical way; they want to teach others the skills they need so they can help themselves.

If you don't have planets in the eleventh house, this is not a negative thing. Not having planets in a house just means that there are no major issues related to that area of life. It is important that you look at the sign on the cusp of the eleventh house to see how that energy will impact your friendships, groups, and goals. For instance, if Pisces is on the house cusp, you will be attracted to creative, artistic, and compassionate people. You might want to join a humanitarian group that helps the homeless or those in need.

If You Have Planets in the Eleventh House

You have a great desire to be part of a group and prefer group work over working alone. Developing lasting friendships with others is key to eleventh-house success. You enjoy making friends and interacting with unique people. Friendship is crucial for your happiness, and having many acquaintances is second nature for you because of your friendly nature. It is important for you to feel accepted and included because you want to connect with others; feeling lonely can cause pain and heartache. Being part of a group brings a sense of cohesiveness that makes you feel supported.

The energy of this house manifests as a mission of service that involves socializing, organizing, and developing connections with a wide range of individuals. You have a giving heart and like helping others on a grand scale. Eleventh-house people are humanitarians, so you find your niche leading a group or serving others in some way. You enjoy working with others toward a common goal, and you should utilize your creative ideas to solve problems.

Creativity and thinking outside the box are important to you, and you have a need to stand out and be seen as different than anyone else. It is important to bring your creative and unconventional ideas into conversations with friends and groups. Planets here enhance intelligence and create revolutionary thinkers who like to challenge other people to open up their minds. You enjoy proving people wrong and showing others that there is always a different way to think about things.

Since Uranus rules the eleventh house, you will most likely be attracted to very unique, rebellious individuals. Planets here attract people who question society and traditional beliefs such as religion. You may want to join unique organizations with a special mission that might even be controversial. Anything that is nontraditional falls under this house, therefore anything that shocks others—such as joining a UFO club, working with AIDS patients, or rallying for animal rights—is embodied by the eleventh house.

You have a sporadic energy that changes easily, making you appear unpredictable. In relationships, you might have difficulty fully committing to others. You do not appreciate feeling like you have to conform or change your behavior for anyone; this makes you feel trapped. If you have to restrict yourself in any way, relationships can feel repressive. If others are too clingy or possessive, you run away and seek space because having freedom to explore and roam is crucial for your overall well-being.

The eleventh house is the house of dreams and visions for the future. You have a strong desire to achieve your hopes, wishes, and dreams. Experiencing synchronicity and attracting what you want in life is an eleventh-house blessing. Believing that you can have what you want is the first step to obtaining desires, goals, relationships, or blessings. Writing out your goals will help connect the dots and you will achieve success through manifestation. It is important for you to reach for the stars and manifest your greatest desires. Believing in yourself, asking the Universe for what you want, and knowing you can have it are the first steps toward manifestation.

Planets in the Eleventh House

If you have one or more planets in the eleventh house, read the corresponding section for tips for transformation, healing, and resilience.

Sun in the Eleventh House

You are a person who enjoys being part of groups and organizations. Having many acquaintances and friendships brings happiness, but be cautious about superficiality and make time to develop deeper friendships.

You have a strong drive to make social changes and impact society in some way, so a career in politics could be beneficial. With this placement, you are known to be socially influential and are able to sway people to your side. You are well suited for humanitarian missions because you like to share a common goal with others. It is important for you to make time to meet people who share similar beliefs. This placement makes it easy for you to focus on the goals of the group versus individual change. Figure out your hopes, wishes, and dreams and make time to pursue the things that bring you happiness.

Moon in the Eleventh House

You are a person who finds emotional comfort in being an integral part of a group. Emotional fulfillment comes from socializing and collaborating with others on projects. Developing friendships with people who share similar values is important for emotional fulfillment. Swaying others to your side with your charming social skills is common with this placement. Humanitarian work that involves caring for and helping others is where you feel most comfortable; helping others in some way helps connect to a greater purpose.

This placement creates a detached emotional and intellectual nature. With the moon here, emotions fluctuate. It is important for you to feel free to act on your emotions, impulses, and intuition. Make time to express your imaginative and creative side through writing, painting, drawing, or playing music.

Mercury in the Eleventh House

You are a person who enjoys communicating and sharing stories. Friendships are an important part of your life, and surrounding yourself with intellectual people brings success. You become bored with people who can't carry a conversation on a vast array of topics. Enjoyment comes from sharing facts and gossiping, but be cautious about sharing too much information with others. Socially influential with an ability to charm others, it is easy to make others believe everything you say. This placement makes you an excellent salesman, teacher, or politician because of your natural public speaking abilities.

Writing down your thoughts in a journal would be beneficial to capture important ideas that cross your mind. Express your creative thoughts by thinking of ways to help humanity and larger groups. Make time to research and find innovative solutions to complex problems. Encourage change and have open-minded conversations with others.

Venus in the Eleventh House

Expressing your artistic and creative talents by joining special groups helps you feel supported. Venus in the eleventh house attracts eccentric, unique, and intellectual types of people. Socializing with groups of people and being seen as polite are important to you. This placement indicates a need to portray a positive face to the world.

You are a person who values friendship over romance. You have to have a mental connection to feel attracted to someone. Learning how to commit to others and develop personal relationships is a great lesson with this placement. Marrying someone who started out as a friend would be a good decision.

Mars in the Eleventh House

You are a person who has a strong drive to lead and be in charge of groups. Happiness comes from challenging rules and creating powerful change. Belonging to a group inspires you to fight for causes that make a larger impact. Passionate and assertive, you can be found championing humanitarian causes and encouraging group members to think and act on solutions. This placement provides natural organizational abilities, which are a huge asset to any team. But be careful not to force your beliefs and opinions on others. Impulsive and aggressive, you can sometimes lose friendships or be removed from groups due to conflict. You fight for causes that powerfully change the lives of others—just be careful not to push people away with your strong passion and direct personality.

Jupiter in the Eleventh House

You are a person who attracts positive friendships and many acquaintances. Jupiter here has an abundance of energy when working in groups and can uplift others with positive energy. Good luck and blessings come from your friends and from belonging to inspirational groups whose purpose is to help others; powerful and wealthy friends often enter your life and assist you as you pursue your goals and dreams.

This placement creates an amazing ability to attract things, so make sure to express gratitude and appreciation. Develop a plan to give financially or emotionally to humanitarian causes. Focus on positive thinking and your natural ability to motivate others. Make time for travel and explore new places with family and friends. Growth comes from expressing your ideas and embracing independence.

Saturn in the Eleventh House

You have a tendency to take friendships seriously, but you may find it difficult to develop friendships with people your own age. Practical and loyal, you expect the same high standards in return. Saturn here prefers spending time with people who are older and more mature.

Superficial conversations make you uncomfortable, and trusting people can be challenging. You fear being hurt by others, which can block your ability to join groups or fully open up to friends. You find it difficult to be vulnerable or share your feelings and beliefs. It takes a lot of time to develop lasting friendships, and you are cautious about who is allowed in your inner circle.

Social situations can be difficult and uncomfortable, which makes it hard to have fun. You are a person who feels restricted and vulnerable in groups. Sometimes you feel like an outsider who doesn't quite belong. It is important to heal karmic insecurities about being a member of a group.

Uranus in the Eleventh House

You are a person who likes to be a part of groups that create change. Unique and eccentric, you need to be a part of humanitarian causes that shake things up and cause growth. With this placement, you might realize that rebelling from groups can sometimes be a good thing. Developing friendships with original and creative people that share similar interests comes naturally.

If you have this placement, friendships can change dramatically throughout life, and there could be many unexpected endings. It is critical to heal issues related to finding stability with reliable friends and groups. Letting go of groups, friends, and acquaintances that are no longer helping you grow is a life lesson.

Neptune in the Eleventh House

It is important to be cautious about which groups or organizations you get involved in, especially those of a spiritual nature. Due to your compassionate, trusting, kind nature, you can be taken advantage of by opportunists. If you do choose to join a group, make sure it matches your spiritual interests and goals.

This placement clouds your vision and causes you to see people as you believe them to be, not as they really are. You are a person who often feels disillusioned by friendships and groups;

surrounding yourself with spiritual friends who share similar ideas brings comfort. Don't give up on what you want, and start believing in yourself. Learn to be more realistic and practical by planning a way to achieve your future goals.

Attracting people who need healing can sometimes be draining, so make time to replenish and rejuvenate your energy. It is important to heal past wounds involving friendship so you attract those who are deserving.

Pluto in the Eleventh House
Sometimes making friends is hard because you have difficulty trusting others or allowing vulnerability. Wounds need to be healed regarding friendship and acceptance. Learning patience and realizing that no one is perfect helps change fears about being hurt. Transformation comes by developing deep, spiritual, and supportive friendships. You are extremely loyal, but this means you can also be possessive. Be careful not to control others.

You are a person who has an intense desire to be part of a powerful group. You actually prefer being the one who has the power to influence group dynamics. Allow yourself to become a leader in groups that you care about and fight for the causes that matter to you. If you are part of a group, you will be able to see the true motives of the members and the leaders.

CHAPTER

Pisces &
the Twelfth House

Nickname: Pisces the Mystic

Symbol: The fish

Sun Sign Dates: February 19–March 20

Ruler: Neptune

Rules: The twelfth house; the feet and pituitary gland

Sign Type: Water, mutable

Polar Opposite Sign: Virgo

Tips for Healing: Avoid escapism, accept reality,
develop boundaries

Pisces is a water sign. It is also a mutable sign, which blesses Pisceans with an easygoing, laid-back, adaptable personality that can change direction at the last minute. Pisceans are known to be compassionate, sensitive, and emotional. As a very empathic, intuitive person, their artistic and creative abilities are heightened. They are sensitive to their environment and absorb all the thoughts, emotions, and energies going on around them. They take on the personality traits, feelings, and beliefs of those they spend time with, so it is important to surround themselves with positive people and avoid negative energy. Pisceans are known to be spiritual and psychic; born intuitive, they often use their psychic abilities to help others.

Out of all the water signs, Pisceans have the deepest understanding of others due to their ability to feel other people's pain. The symbolism of the two fish shows that there is a lack of boundaries; Pisces are born with no armor to protect themselves. The other two water signs, Cancer and Scorpio, are lucky to both have a way to protect themselves: Cancer has its hard crab shell, and Scorpio has the sting of the scorpion that can kill on impact. But Pisceans lack protection, and sometimes they suffer from depression because of their sensitive nature.

CHALLENGING ATTRIBUTES OF A PISCES

When they experience difficult times, Pisceans ignore their own feelings and emotions for the greater good or for those they care about. They need to make it a priority to spend time alone to recharge. Sometimes Pisceans do not understand if what they are feeling is coming from the environment, other people, or from within, and spending time alone can help them figure that out. If they do not have time to be alone to recover from day-to-day activities, they can become moody, irritable, depressed, and anxious.

Pisceans' health can suffer if strong boundaries are not developed early in life, especially when it comes to interacting with unhealthy people. An important lesson for Pisceans to learn is to say no to others while listening to their intuitive instinct. This helps avoid heartbreak and prevents them from being taken advantage of.

Disillusionment and suffering come when Pisceans see selfishness, harshness, and unkindness in the world, and when they witness how people treat each other. When other people let them down, it can take a long time for Pisceans to recover and heal. Pisceans see people with rose-colored glasses, and their giving nature often turns into sacrifice. This sign is known for sacrificing their own financial stability and emotional comfort for people they care about, and this can be their greatest weakness.

Pisceans have a need to escape from the world and sometimes avoid living in the real world by isolating themselves. This sign rules addiction; Pisceans need to be extra careful not to overindulge in alcohol, drugs, food, sex, or anything that numbs their pain or shuts off their emotions.

Positive Attributes of a Pisces

The planet Neptune rules Pisces, creating a strong need to avoid unpleasant thoughts, emotions, and experiences. Pisceans expect other people to be as compassionate as they are, often putting people on a pedestal. Because they are naturally kind and sympathetic, it's important for Pisceans to take care of their emotional needs and develop healthy coping skills. It is important to embrace their need to withdraw and to pursue solitary activities that help them feel better.

Pisceans are one of the most spiritual signs of the zodiac. Having faith and believing in a higher power brings them strength in times of crisis. Since they were children, Pisceans have sought answers to the meaning of life and why they are here. They believe it's their duty to serve others in some capacity, and their partners and friends are drawn to their empathic nature. Pisceans' compassionate and spiritual energy attracts people who have experienced pain and suffering. Feeling other people's pain can be a blessing and a curse; developing boundaries will ensure that they can help others without neglecting themselves in the process.

Pisces rules the twelfth astrological house. Issues such as spirituality, escapism, secrets, suffering, service to others, meditation, and cosmic consciousness are associated with this house. Spiritual practices such as meditation, yoga, deep breathing, energy healing, and alternative medicine attract Pisceans. Born with an active imagination, Pisceans naturally experience visions and dream deeply.

Pisces enjoys expressing their artistic talents by playing music, drawing, and writing. Tapping into their creativity and immersing themselves in music motivates Pisceans. Fulfillment comes when they are able to fully express themselves with others and have spiritual, kind, compassionate friends to connect with and confide in. The emotional intensity of Pisces enables them to help others deeply, but they need to be careful not to lose themselves in the process. Pisceans' greatest lessons are to develop boundaries, listen to their intuition, and live a spiritual life.

Relationships with a Pisces

Pisceans befriend people who need help, people who have been rejected by others, and people who have been abandoned. They spend hours trying to help other people, but this can leave them feeling drained if they don't get the same care in return. Pisceans need to be careful whom they let into their life and surround themselves with positive people. Learning to balance their kind and giving nature will keep them from focusing all their healing energy on others. It is critical to spend time alone, as it will help balance their physical and mental health. When they learn to take care of themselves first, they will feel happier.

When it comes to love and relationships, experiencing heartbreak is common. Pisceans seek a spiritual lover and soul mate they can depend on, but they often have difficulty finding the right partner. They are known to be romantic and mystical and easily taken advantage of by others. Romance may lead to suffering because of their extreme idealistic tendencies, especially if they ignore their intuition and instincts. They should always check in with their intuition before committing to someone. Pisceans can attract people who are unhealthy or emotionally unstable, and this can make them feel emotionally abused, manipulated, and used. Stepping back, being more practical, and seeing people clearly without romanticizing them will help in the long run.

Pisces Tips for Transformation

Pisceans transform when they learn that they can balance their spiritual gifts and their health. There is a natural desire to escape from the world and responsibilities. If Pisceans can overcome the tendency to withdraw, they can transform into stronger individuals. Finding a good balance between pursuing hobbies and handling real-world issues can help them adapt to change or crisis. Balancing stress and unpleasant emotions will help overall health and well-being.

Love Yourself

Pisceans always give to others who are suffering, but this can be painful and lead to burnout. They transform when they realize that people with problems and unhealed pain are attracted to them, so setting boundaries is crucial to their well-being. Pisceans need to learn to focus on giving more attention and love to themselves instead of sacrificing or neglecting their own needs. They often struggle with self-esteem concerns due to their sensitive nature. They heal by finding self-love. Learning self-love means valuing and accepting their flaws. They tend to be hard on themselves, and they do not always see themselves clearly. Pisceans need to show the same kindness to themselves that they so freely give to others. Learning to embrace their creative side can help them express emotions and connect with their inner desires. Meditation, writing in a journal, or studying crystals, astrology, and metaphysical topics can be tools to help increase a Piscean's sense of purpose and self-love.

Conserve Your Energy

Selfless personality traits can be draining, so Pisceans need to be careful about how much energy they give to others. Spending time alone energizes them so they can reemerge stronger and more prepared. The only reason Pisceans want to escape from the world is so they can find peace, connection, and comfort; activities that help conserve energy such as reading, art, writing, listening to music, and meditating are beneficial for healing. It is transforming for Pisceans to withdraw from social situations and family obligations to recharge. Social situations and groups can deplete their energy, and it is important that family and friends understand this.

Develop Boundaries

It is difficult for Pisceans to turn people away because they always try to please others. They transform when they learn to develop stronger boundaries in relationships. Setting boundaries is important, especially when helping other people with their problems. Boundaries actually give Pisceans the strength to decipher what other people truly need—they will be able to focus on their intuition if they've worked on taking care of themselves first.

PISCES TIPS FOR HEALING

It is important for Pisceans to spend time alone each day. Privacy is critical for overcoming anxiety, depression, and stress. Doing enormous amounts of selfless acts comes easier when they are centered, energized, and grounded.

Spend Time with Animals

Owning pets can bring healing and companionship. Animals serve as therapy pets for Pisceans and help nourish their soul, and giving unconditional love comes naturally to a Pisces. Loving connections with animals can help Pisceans survive the most difficult times in life.

Nurture Your Spiritual Connection

Pisceans find comfort in spiritual art and peaceful music. Finding a spiritual connection is the most important mission for

Pisceans. They might be drawn to angels and enjoy collecting icons. Believing that someone is watching over them and ensuring their safety helps Pisceans go out into the world with a greater sense of purpose. Whether they are drawn to angels or not, Pisceans tend to surround themselves with mystical and spiritual decorations.

Pisceans need to incorporate spiritual techniques and routines into their lives, such as meditation, prayer, yoga, and breathing exercises. They benefit from studying different religious beliefs and philosophies. Making time to connect with a higher power will help them when they experience loss. Spending time in contemplation in a peaceful environment also helps the healing process.

Compassionately Serve

The world needs Pisceans; they are a shining light to those who are stuck in the darkness, struggling without hope. Pisceans are destined to compassionately serve others and take care of those in pain. Their kind, sympathetic, nurturing nature gives others hope. Pisceans are truly angels on earth who wander around healing everyone who crosses their path, and allowing their angelic light to shine is important. They are able to truly help others because they have experienced pain and know what it feels like to be sad, depressed, or alone.

Sleep Regularly

Vulnerable areas for Pisceans are the feet and lymphatic system. Injuries to the feet, toes, and arches are common. Pisceans are sensitive to colds, viruses, and infections because their immune system is extremely vulnerable in stressful environments. They are known to need more sleep than other signs, and a healthy sleep schedule is crucial for their well-being. Maintaining a good work-life balance is also important because excessive stress can cause mental confusion and depression. Getting enough sleep will help balance overall health.

Pisces Resiliency

Pisceans are mystical healers. Life can feel very lonely sometimes, but loneliness helps them become more resilient because it reminds them of their mission to help others. They often feel like no one understands them until they find their spiritual circle; they become more resilient when they find other people who share similar interests. It is important to find a deep connection with something outside of themselves.

Pisceans are here for a purpose, and sometimes this purpose is forced upon them. The biggest lesson they have to learn is to let go and trust the spiritual laws of the Universe. Sometimes the Universe strips away things that Pisceans love and cherish as a lesson in becoming more mystical and spiritually gifted. There may be times when Pisceans don't understand why something happened the way it did, but having faith helps them overcome these emotions. When struggling with crises or unpleasant situations, Pisceans rise up stronger if they're focused on a spiritual path.

Focusing on finding deeper meaning and embracing mystical experiences helps them realize that everything happens for a reason. Pisceans need to remember that the Universe has a plan for their lives. Feeling a mystical connection to spirit is what helps them connect with other people, God, and humanity. To feel true oneness seems like a daunting task, but Pisceans are more equipped to succeed at it than any other sign.

How to Support a Pisces

If there is a Pisces in your life, encourage their compassionate spirit and open-minded attitude. Encourage them to trust their instincts and psychic intuition. Accept their deeply emotional nature and let them communicate their feelings openly, without criticism or judgment. Be pure and kind when connecting with them. Support their dreams and artistic talents. Spend quality time together listening to music, meditating, and cuddling.

Pisces Reflection Questions

- What helps you when you're sad and depressed?
- How can you develop stronger boundaries?
- Is there anything you need to heal?
- What personality traits help you become more resilient?
- How do you handle stress and anxiety?

Pisces Affirmations

- "I am worthy of love. I give myself the same amount of love I give to others."
- "I listen to my needs. Alone time helps me recharge."
- "I enjoy helping and healing others. I make time to heal myself as well. I engage in activities that soothe my soul."
- "My spirituality is a priority. Connection to my spiritual side heals me."

PISCES SELF-CARE IDEAS

- Sit in silence. Meditate, breathe, and focus on being still.

- Draw, paint, play music, and spend time in nature.

- Go on a boat ride, surf, or canoe. Water is healing.

- Create three positive affirmations to recite daily.

- List three self-care techniques you find helpful and make time to do those things.

- Draw a flower with seven petals. Write down one new self-care activity you want to implement in each of the petals. Then hang the flower on the wall as a reminder. Try to do one new self-care activity every day until you've incorporated them into your routine.

THE TWELFTH HOUSE

Imagine feeling God's presence touch your heart and soul. Some individuals are lucky enough to feel this, and most of them probably have a few planets in the twelfth house. This is the most spiritual house in a birth chart; the twelfth house blesses us with psychic and mystical experiences. This is also the house of escapism, secrets, compassion, karma, cosmic consciousness, loneliness, service to others, suffering, psychological issues, and sacrifice.

I like to describe this house as a blessing and a curse because there are many deeply emotional experiences that happen when planets are placed here. On the other hand, the twelfth house helps us connect deeply with humanity and with the environment. When there are planets in the twelfth house, emotions are powerful and life is deeply understood. There is also a strong urge to be alone and spend time in isolation. The energy of this house is turned inward and creates a secluded, reclusive, private type of person who seeks the meaning of life.

Twelfth-house planets create a magnetic field that attracts wounded souls. People that need healing or comfort are drawn to those with twelfth-house planets. We can thank the sign Pisces for this great gift, the ruler of the twelfth house. Pisces is the mystic, the spiritualist, the escapist, and the compassionate one.

If you don't have planets in the twelfth house, this is not a negative thing. It simply means that there are no major life issues impacting this area of your life. You will want to look at the sign that is on the cusp of the twelfth house to see what energy impacts this area of your life. For instance, if Pisces is on the twelfth house cusp, you might feel a lack of boundaries between yourself and others. You have a desire to help those who have problems, so you are drawn to the helping professions. Alone time, seclusion, and privacy will be important for your mental and spiritual health. Seeking a connection with a higher power will be paramount.

If You Have Planets in the Twelfth House

You often suffer with issues surrounding personal boundaries. When there is a lack of protection, you are left wide open to feel all of the negativity, sadness, and unhappiness around you. If someone cries, tears swell up inside your eyes and you cry too. Absorbing people's pain makes you a great spiritual healer, but this is why it is crucial to develop boundaries. If you don't have strong boundaries, you are left with a deep desire to numb your emotions because the twelfth house forces you to feel everything. It is important to avoid escaping through drugs and alcohol because you are physically, mentally, and spiritually sensitive to substances.

The twelfth house is shrouded in mystery. You are able to help others understand secrets, hidden things, and illusions. It is important to understand that the twelfth house is the most spiritual house in the astrological chart. When planets are placed in the twelfth house, there are inherited intuitive abilities that often come from a maternal or paternal grandparent. From a young age, you've seen things that can't be explained, such as ghosts. Having vivid dreams about the future is common with planets here. Your mystical experiences may even be a daily experience. These experiences reinforce your natural shyness and create a desire to keep things secret from others. You may feel like you do not belong on earth; this feeling often develops at a young age. You may wonder why you are so different than others and feel like an alien. You may struggle to fit in with your family members or people your own age. Always feeling like an outsider looking in is a common twelfth-house experience.

The twelfth house encourages you to seek a connection and cure for your loneliness. Reaching out to God, the Creator, or Source will give you a sense of belonging and protection. Spiritual experiences help confirm your belief in a higher power. Through meditation and prayer, you can find peace within yourself. It is important to remember that when you are suffering, relief can be found in seeking a connection through spiritual pursuits. Finding time to meditate and detach from the physical realm brings peace and tranquility. Spending time studying topics such as astrology, tarot, occultism, and metaphysics can comfort you and help you make sense of powerful experiences.

When planets are in this house, peace of mind comes through meditation, alone time, withdrawing, journaling, reading, and doing activities in isolation. In large groups, it is common for you to experience a sense of detachment from your physical body or a loss of boundaries. For you, being alone is not just a desire—it is a necessity. If you don't have a space in your home where you can get away or find quiet time, this will make you irritable or sad. It is important to find time to recharge so you can grow and heal.

You are extremely sensitive to other people's feelings and thoughts; you can sense what others truly feel. You are compassionate, caring, and self-sacrificing. You enjoy serving others in some way because of your ability to empathize. You are giving and like to feel helpful. Serving those in need attracts you to helping professions like psychology, counseling, social work, and spiritual work. You are an excellent counselor who cares about other people's problems because of your inborn kindness. You are a bright light in the darkness, and you bless the lives of others everywhere you go. Because of this, you attract others who have problems. At times, it may feel like you have a sign on your back that says "Come to me for healing." Psychic sensitivity is high, and you must learn to protect yourself by avoiding negative people who like to take without giving back in return. Learning how to conserve your energy and giving only to those who appreciate your kindness are major lessons.

It is important for you not to let your kindness become a curse. You need to develop a good balance when it comes to selflessness or you could get taken advantage of, even by those you trust. This is why the twelfth house is called the house of suffering. You might feel used, tossed out, abandoned, or betrayed several times in your life. This happens because you tend to only see the good in other people, often ignoring red flags. The fact is that most people are nothing like you; they are incapable of the kind of love and sacrifice that you share every day. You are an angel on earth, a fallen angel wandering here with a special mission, and that is the important mission of service.

PLANETS IN THE TWELFTH HOUSE

If you have one or more planets in the twelfth house, read the corresponding section for tips for transformation, healing, and resiliency.

Sun in the Twelfth House

You are a person who enjoys escaping from the world and secluding yourself. Spending time alone is critical for your peace of mind. Having a peaceful and harmonious environment helps create comfort and safety. This placement shows an extremely sensitive and spiritual person who is drawn to the hidden and mystical side of life. Secretive by nature, there is a tendency to hide your true personality or identity from others. Control your escapist tendencies by embracing your psychic abilities and spiritual gifts.

You experience strong emotions that can lead to depression, sadness, and anxiety. You feel different from most people, which leads you to avoid groups. You also don't feel comfortable around most people. You find fulfillment in helping others, but be cautious about attracting people who have problems because it is second nature for you to help them while neglecting your own needs. Develop stronger boundaries in your relationships, and accept that you might always feel lonely. It is part of your journey of finding out who you truly are.

Healing your relationship with your father figure or coming to terms with the lack of support you received will help you transform.

Moon in the Twelfth House

You are a person who has a very spiritual and psychic emotional nature. Still waters run deep, and hiding your emotions is a protective mechanism that you use to avoid being hurt. Sometimes trusting others too easily can make you feel taken advantage of. You need time to withdraw from the world to recharge and balance your emotions. Listening to soothing music brings comfort during times of stress. Making time to journal your thoughts and feelings will help you express your emotions. Healing your emotional wounds will make you a powerful, spiritual person.

As a natural healer, people with pain are drawn to you, and helping them brings emotional fulfillment. It is important to listen to your intuitive, perceptive, and insightful feelings because you are able to see the truth that others like to hide. You have an interest in psychology and social work because you enjoy helping others with their problems. But others' energy affects your mood, so it's good to surround yourself with positive people.

Healing the relationship with your mother and overcoming feeling responsible for her happiness will help you grow.

Mercury in the Twelfth House

You are a deep thinker and often hide your true thoughts. It is sometimes difficult for you to express your feelings. Shyness can get in the way, making it difficult to tell others what you think. Focus on communicating and expressing your thoughts, and make time to share your intuitive ideas with others.

When Mercury is here, your first impressions are accurate. You almost have an ability to read other people's minds. Flashes of intuition and creative ideas come out of the blue, so it's important to carry a journal to write them down. Because you are private and secretive about your inner world, you could benefit from writing, journaling, painting, or drawing. Spending time alone to recover from daily life, quieting the mind, and daydreaming help you deal with stress.

Venus in the Twelfth House
You are secretive and hide your true romantic feelings. This placement is an indicator of suffering through love affairs and heartache at some time in life. Sometimes falling in love with someone who is unavailable is a karmic lesson. Try not to idealize other people and work on seeing them clearly. Transform your fantasies about love by learning to be more realistic and practical.

The positive energy of this placement is that you are protected by guardian angels. This placement often attracts people who need healing. Helping others is important, but make sure not to let others take advantage of your kindness. It is important for you to take care of your own needs too. Venus here can cause feelings of loneliness and a belief that you can't depend on others to be there when you need them. Developing strong, healthy boundaries helps protect your own energy. Recognize that not all people belong in your life, and allow people who reciprocate into your inner circle. Expressing your creative and artistic talents helps you heal and transform.

Mars in the Twelfth House

You are a person who has strong intuitive and psychic abilities. Mars here causes an internalization of intense feelings and makes it hard for you to express your emotions outwardly. When you turn emotions like anger inward, it can cause health problems.

You have trouble figuring out what you want and need from others. Sometimes this placement makes you feel like your actions are influenced by forces outside of yourself. Escaping from painful experiences is one way you deal with problems, but it is dangerous to become involved with alcohol, drugs, or other self-destructive behaviors. It is more important to face problems head on. Don't blame yourself or others for everything that happens.

Realize that depression is a natural part of life and something that can be overcome. Overcoming loneliness by seeking a spiritual connection can help create greater healing. Mars here has a complex emotional nature, and benefits come from writing, journaling, and meditation. If you channel your anger into reaching spiritual goals and serving others, transformation will occur. Practice loving yourself and make time to do things you're passionate about.

Jupiter in the Twelfth House

You are a person who is blessed with intuitive abilities and visions that predict the future. Keep a journal next to your bed at night so you can write down your dreams. Connecting easily to spirit, you are blessed with a deep connection to God and might be interested in becoming a nun, priest, or rabbi. Studying ancient knowledge and pursuing things that are mystical and meaningful brings contentment. This placement suggests that a guardian angel watches over your life and protects you from pain and suffering. You are shielded from negativity and protected from the more negative energies of this house.

You have a vivid imagination and an optimistic approach to life. Seeing the good in others comes naturally with Jupiter here, and you will benefit from doing any type of spiritual work. Make time to travel to overseas locations and visit ancient historic sites. Transformation occurs when you give to others and help them heal their wounds. Make sure to spend time alone to explore your own emotional depths.

Saturn in the Twelfth House
You are a person who represses your intuitive nature. This placement might cause fear and doubt when it comes to the spiritual world, and this can test your beliefs. It is important that you stop doubting and embrace your psychic abilities while learning how to use them in a practical way. Do not be afraid to believe in a higher power, and develop your faith to heal karmic spiritual wounds.

This placement can cause feelings of guilt and rigid behaviors that create unpleasant and repressed emotions. You might suffer from depression and sadness, although you work hard to cover it up. You are a master at hiding your true feelings from those you care about. Spending time alone helps heal things, but be cautious about isolating yourself. When Saturn is here, you may suffer from some type of addiction at some point in life, but you are able to overcome it through discipline and willpower.

Even though you do not like relying on others for support, you are the person that family and friends turn to for strength and understanding. Being of service to others helps you break free from unpleasant burdens and destroys the chains that you impose on yourself.

Uranus in the Twelfth House

You are a person who experiences visions of the future. Gifted with intuition and clairvoyance, experiencing flashes of insight and an awareness of upcoming events is common. Trust your visions, dreams, and feelings about the future, and allow the Universe to send messages that help you uplift yourself and others.

Your spiritual beliefs about the world will constantly be challenged and changed. You need freedom to explore spiritual topics, and alone time is crucial because it helps you expand the mind. Living in an environment that allows freedom and open-minded discussions will create growth. This placement shows a talent for writing, which brings a sense of peace and helps balance your restless nature. Make time to express your unique, creative abilities by doing things that challenge the mind and society.

This placement can cause suffering due to instability and a rebellious nature. Be cautious about a need to escape by using substances such as alcohol and drugs. Also be cautious about attracting unpredictable and unreliable romantic partners.

Neptune in the Twelfth House

You are extremely compassionate. You are extremely sensitive to the emotions in your environment; you are like a psychic sponge, absorbing everything. You easily pick up on what others think, feel, and believe. But feeling the pain of the world can lead to suffering, feelings of depression, and sadness. This placement indicates that you need to learn how to develop stronger boundaries with others.

You are easily fooled by others who want to drain your positive energy, and you need to work on seeing people clearly. Healing relationship wounds and disappointments will help you grow stronger as a person.

A loner at heart, you prefer to spend time by yourself. Imaginative, creative, and artistic, you can create beautiful things that help you cope with loneliness. Music brings comfort and helps heal you from the stresses of the world. Escaping through drugs and alcohol is not a good solution; finding other outlets to cope with things will benefit many areas of your life.

This placement encourages an ability to connect to God through meditation, prayer, and journaling. Your life will be happiest when you follow a spiritual path. Find your spiritual support group and spend time with them.

Pluto in the Twelfth House

This placement indicates psychic abilities and a deep understanding about life. Deeply secretive, you prefer working behind the scenes and privately doing what you want. Powerful positions draw you out of the dark and into the light. No one truly realizes the power you have in this world and the great healing potential you possess.

You are a person who hides your powerful feelings. Bottling up emotions and keeping them secret from others can lead to escapism. With Pluto here, feeling anger intensely sometimes turns into a rage that you try to repress and hide. Make sure to express your powerful emotions in healthy ways; otherwise, you could suffer from health problems. As a passionate person, you enjoy taking risks to feel alive, but be careful about getting involved in drugs or alcohol, as addiction is common with this placement. Seeking time alone to meditate, write, and think about spiritual issues can help heal negative emotions.

Engaging in passionate love affairs that you keep private from those closest to you is common with this placement. Pluto here can cause an addiction to love and unstable emotional bonds because of difficulties ending unhealthy relationships.

CONCLUSION

Your sun sign offers a variety of tools to help you heal, transform, and find greater resilience. Change is inevitable in life, but how you respond to change is the key to success. After reading your own sun sign chapter and the sections about your birth chart's houses, I hope you were able to learn specific information that will be useful in the future. Determining your comfort level with the information in this book is the first step.

I hope you found these tips and personality profiles validating and helpful in your healing process. I also hope you feel inspired to implement more self-care activities in your routine. Self-care is important for recharging, and it's crucial to pay attention to the needs of your mind, body, and spirit. Daily self-care activities, no matter how simple, help create muscle memory for you to stay on track. When you take good care of yourself and develop a routine, then you are able to live a more balanced life.

In the future when you experience one of life's changes, challenges, or struggles, please remember that you are never alone.

Learning to ask for help is a strength, not a weakness. There are spiritual resources available in your local community and online. Astrology is just one tool that can be used to better understand ourselves and others. I wish you the best of luck on your healing journey.